# A PARENT PRIVILEGE

*That the next generation might know...*

Psalm 78:6

My Family

Steve Wright
with Chris Graves

ApParent Privilege
Copyright © 2008 by Steve Wright

ISBN 978-1-931548-73-1

Available from InQuest.org, Amazon.com, CreateSpace.com, and other retail outlets.

Cover design by Amy Torcasso.
Layout by Metro Productions.
Edited by Kevin Harvey.
Printed in the United States.
2008 First Edition
2010 Second Edition
2014 Third Edition

To Sara, William, and Tyler:
It is a true privilege being your dad.

# TABLE OF CONTENTS

# ACKNOWLEDGEMENTS

It is humbling to see the amount of time and effort given by so many people to make this book a reality. Steve and Chris would first like to acknowledge their wives (Tina and Anne) and the rest of their families for their constant support, selfless sacrifice and humbling tolerance of late nights and long phone calls. They would also like to thank those who have worked directly on the book to make it possible, including Mike Seaver for helping us make sure the book was God-honoring and Gospel-centered, Kristie Melvin and Diana Mattix for proofreading the book, and everyone at the InQuest office for their hard work.

Steve would also like to thank all of those who have helped shape his understanding of what the Bible teaches about family and ministry, including Randy Stinson, Jimmy Scroggins, Allen Jackson, Johnny Derouen, and the incredible pastors at Providence who have invested their lives as men who truly care for others' souls.

# FOREWORD

My family loves the Olympics. We applaud the competition, marvel at the incredible achievements, and enjoy the numerous background stories shared by the media in between competitions. The sacrifices that these athletes make in order to prepare themselves for this experience are staggering. Yet one thing stands out above everything else: the desire for victory. Every athlete is competing to win.

This is part of the point being made in Hebrews 12 as the author uses competition imagery to teach us something:

> Therefore, since we are surrounded by so great a cloud of witnesses, let us also lay aside every weight, and sin which clings so closely, and let us run with endurance the race that is set before us, looking to Jesus, the founder and perfecter of our faith, who for the joy that was set before him endured the cross, despising the shame, and is seated at the right hand of the throne of God. (vv. 1-2)

The expectation in these verses is that the runner is looking for victory; it is the reason he is racing. There will be some striving, contending, enduring, and persevering in the process, but these things are necessary for true gospel living. Paul uses similar athletic imagery when telling Timothy, "Train yourself for godliness; for while bodily training is of some value, godliness is of value in every way, as it holds promise for the present life and also for the life to come" (1 Timothy 4:7-8).

Over the last seventeen years of ministry, I have been saddened by watching parents endure, strive, sacrifice, and contend—for all of the wrong things when it comes to their children. Some of these pursuits are of "some value," but the cultivation of godliness which "is of value in every way" gets the least amount of attention. Paul is not saying there should be no bodily training. Rather, he is challenging you and me to bring the same type of commitment and motivation to work hard to the task of spiritual growth. Parents should bring more energy, willingness to sacrifice, and inclination for endurance to the task of their children's discipleship than to any other parenting responsibility. Paul is telling us that eternal things are at stake. We are to treat our responsibilities with the appropriate level of seriousness.

The book you hold in your hand will help you in that task. Two years ago, Steve Wright began challenging youth ministry leaders to rethink youth ministry. As a result, parents are being asked to embrace the primary responsibility of discipling their own children. This idea has created a genuine movement in the evangelical community to which parents are responding, "How?" Well, Steve has served us once again by giving parents some biblical, theological, and practical instruction on how they might begin to assert themselves in this role and be effective in leading their children to become authentic followers of Christ.

My friendship with Steve Wright was instantaneous, not because of our mutual love for baseball or our years of Christian ministry but because of our deep and abiding burden for families. We both think about families when we get up, when we go to bed, and when we are woken up in the middle of the night. What you are about to read is authentic. Steve is the real deal, and I am confident that if you put into practice the content of this book, your family will be encouraged to exalt Christ and follow Him. Hearts of fathers will be turned toward their children, and hearts of children will be turned toward their fathers. These are the evidences of the manifest presence of God in the home. This discipleship is where you should invest your time and energy. Contend and strive for this process. Endure in it because it "holds promise for this life and also for the life to come."

Randy Stinson, Ph.D.

Dean, School of Leadership and Church Ministry,
The Southern Baptist Theological Seminary

President, The Council on Biblical Manhood
and Womanhood

# INTRODUCTION

Recently, I had a sobering conversation with Frank, a fifty-six-year-old man who has faithfully sought to walk with the Lord for decades. Everyone would label Frank's family as core members of their church. His family rarely missed a Wednesday or Sunday. They were active in numerous ministries. His church had what was considered an excellent and active youth ministry, and he made sure his children were there. They thought they were doing all the right things.

Frank told me, "Steve, as my wife and I were raising our boys I realize that we believed that our job was to bring our boys to church. We truly believed that if we could find a good youth program and keep our children active, then they would continue to serve Christ. We realize now that this belief system, no matter how earnestly we believed it, did not hold true for us. Our two adult children now in their thirties are no longer walking with Christ. We brought them to church, dropped them off at their program, and ran off to serve in other places, all the while honestly believing we were doing the right thing. I wish that someone had told us that the responsibility of discipling our children was ours, not a pastor's. I wish we would have known."

Frank's story is all too common. We now see around two-thirds of young people leaving the church around the time of graduation. Two-thirds of children in church-going families, like Frank's, are walking away from Christ. This alarming number of young people becoming prodigals and the countless conversations I have had with parents like Frank is why I am writing this book.

I have a vested interest in this topic. I am a dad of three teenage children—Sara, William, and Tyler—so I write this book to you, as one parent to another. I have also been a student pastor for over twenty years, so I have a unique seat as I talk with many parents and pastors all over the country. I believe that most parents know deep down that they cannot hand the privilege of discipling their children to a pastor. This book will show parents why the Bible says they are primary.

I write this book for you—parents—to encourage you, to inspire you, to equip you, and to resource you. I also write as a dad with great concerns about the world in which we live, but with great hope in the Gospel. You have an incredible privilege plainly in front of you, the apparent privilege to disciple your children. I pray that this book strengthens you in your task.

# A Parent's Concern: Are They Listening?

On October 4, 1991, the doctor placed Sara in my awkwardly awaiting arms. She had been born just moments before, and in those first moments my life had changed completely. I became a parent.

Sara was bundled like a seven-pound-eleven-ounce cocoon holding a delicate butterfly. I can still remember feeling her first gentle breaths against my neck as I took her and held her close. Then *it* happened. In an instant, I fell in love with someone I had just met, and my life took a new direction. I vowed then and there that I would do anything for her. I would do whatever it took to protect and provide for her, understanding that God had placed an eternal soul in my care. You are reading this book today because you made a similar vow. We willingly made these vows realizing the great privilege we have been entrusted with—every parent's privilege.

Imagine what those first moments were like for our children. These fragile little infants were thrust into a new world, a world where they completely depended on their parents who were learning as they went along. My wife, Tina, and I cared for Sara, along with her younger brothers, William and Tyler, in the coming years, the best way we knew how, but we realized we were learning as much as our kids were. We became schooled in everything about diapers, bottles, and pacifiers. We became fluent in babyese and toddler talk. We memorized Dr. Seuss's *Foot Book* and knew all about "The Wheels on the Bus." We learned how to carry from the car all three kids, diaper bags, and everything we needed for church in one trip. My wife, my kids, and I were in this together—late nights and early mornings, toothless grins and temper tantrums—each of us ill prepared for the task at hand and each of us learning along the way, trying to keep a focus on the eternal while the immediate needs were tireless.

If you are a parent, then you too have shared some of the same thoughts of inadequacy, feeling both under-equipped and overwhelmed. My kids aren't the little ones they once were; I now have three teenagers in my house. While their ages and situations have changed, the feelings of inadequacy that we all sense as parents have not. As our children grow, we continue to doubt ourselves, our skills, and our ability to impact their lives. Amid all of the cultural influences, peer influences, and media influences, often our influences seem to erode as we feel like we take a place in line behind dozens of others who influence our children. In these years, many parents believe that kids listen to their friends, celebrities, trendsetters, schoolteachers, leaders at church, and just about anyone else more than they listen to mom and dad. We feel shoved to the bottom of the list of those who determine the direction our children will take. We begin to hear voices saying things like, "We can't relate to them like we used to." "They don't think we are cool anymore." "They just don't listen to us." Or so we think.

While you may feel inadequate and may think that your kids stopped listening years ago, you may be surprised by the facts. The latest research and time-tested biblical precepts emphasize the exact opposite. Your children listen to you. They both want and need you involved in their lives. You have an apparent privilege, the most exciting of your life, right in front of you—to be a touch of grace on your children's souls.

## Apparent Facts

For years parents have bought into a lie that the greatest influences in their children's lives are peers, media, and others outside of the home. It's just not true. There seems to be professionals everywhere—professional teachers, professional nannies, professional counselors, and professional church staff. Many of us have come to see a great divide between the trained professionals and ordinary, untrained mom and dad. With so many plates spinning and parents' weakened confidence that we are even qualified for parenting, we do what the culture applauds: we leave much of the parenting to professionals. This conventional wisdom says to enroll your kids in the best schools to handle their educational development; get them on the right team in the right league to handle their athletic development; find a great counselor to handle their emotional development; and find the best church where we can drop off our kids to handle their spiritual development. So what is left for parents to do? Handle their child's basic needs and hope that everyone else is doing their job? How misguided! Research is showing us that this makes as much sense as rearranging the deck furniture on the *Titanic*. Children are listening! Parents still have the greatest influence on their children.

Today we have unparalleled access to information and research about parenting, and it shouts so loudly that it cannot be ignored. Listen to the extent to which kids listen to their moms and dads:

- An extensive study of 272,400 teenagers conducted by *USA Today Weekend Magazine* found that 70 percent of teens identified their parents as the most important influence in their lives. Twenty-one percent said that about their friends (peers), and only 8 percent named the media.[1]

- MVParents.com says, "Nearly three out of four parents believe their children's friends and classmates have the most influence. . . . Yet contrary to what parents think, kids say mom and dad have the biggest impact on the choices they make."[2]

- In a national survey, 1,129 middle school students were asked what the greatest influence in their life was, and parents topped the list. The results were: parents—37 percent, friends—22 percent, church—11 percent, youth pastor—7 percent, and music—5 percent. Adult volunteers, schoolteachers, culture, and the Internet each scored 2 percent or less. A national survey of 923 high school students yielded very similar results. [3]

- MTV and the Associated Press released a study on influence of parents that said, "So you're between the ages of 13 and 24. What makes you happy? A worried, weary parent might imagine the answer to sound something like this: Sex, drugs, and a little rock 'n' roll. Maybe some cash, or at least the car keys. Turns out the real an¬swer is quite different. Spend¬ing time with family was the top answer to that open-ended question. . . . Parents are seen as an overwhelmingly posi¬tive influence in the lives of most young people. Remarkably, near¬ly half of teens mention at least one of their parents as a hero."[4]

- An Anheuser-Busch Web site supports this logic, saying, "Studies have shown that parents are the primary influence on their children's choices and decisions . . . and that is why we're proud to offer help to parents." [5]

- After years of secular research, Bob Altemeyer and Bruce Hunsberger say, "We acquire our religion from our parents almost as certainly as we inherit the color of our eyes." [6] (Don't misunderstand. They're not saying that faith is genetic, but they are saying that parents have more influence on faith than any other person).

- Altemeyer and Hunsberger also say, "All of the different approaches to studying parental influences in the religious socialization process converge on a single conclu¬sion: Parents play an extremely important role in the developing religious attitudes and practices of their offspring. In fact, few re¬searchers would quarrel with the conclusion that parents are the most important influence in this regard."[7]

- Researchers Merton Strommen and Richard Hardel say, "We conclude our research by reiterating that the family is the most powerful institution in promoting faith in youth. The family atmosphere allows children to enter into a love relationship with God. We say this out of a conviction that congregations have erred in allowing the focus of faith development to shift from the home to the congregation or parish."[8]

Remember that this is *secular* research pointing to the importance of parents. These studies obviously contradict cultural misconceptions that peers and media are the primary driving force for young people. Parents have that distinction. Josh McDowell sums it up perfectly: "Parents . . . carry more weight—for good or bad—than they give themselves credit for."[9]

## APPARENT WISDOM

You don't, however, have to look to research groups to
see the influence that parents have. It is as if God Himself
personally whispered His instruction into your ear, etched
it on your heart, and impressed it on your soul; His guidance has been calling out clearly for thousands of years
in His Word. This eternal truth constantly emphasizes,
empowers, and validates our privilege as parents. Think
about why. Why are parents commanded over and over
again to talk to their children about spiritual things? It's
because children listen to their parents—God wrote this on
their hearts. If God knew that we had no influence on our
kids, the Bible would have no reason to tell us parents to
spend time teaching our children. Here is just a glimpse of
what the Bible says:

- Exodus 10:2 shares the importance of passing down
  the faith, saying, "That you may tell in the hearing of
  your son and grandson [the things I have done] . . .
  that you may know that I am the LORD."

- Exodus 12:26–28 speaks of explaining the symbols of
  the faith to your children when they ask (the Passover
  in context).

- Deuteronomy 11:19 commands, "Teach [God's words]
  to your children, talking of them when you are sitting
  in your house, and when you are walking by the way,
  and when you lie down, and when you rise."

- Joshua 24:15 says, "Choose this day whom you will serve. . . . But as for me and my house, we will serve the LORD."

- Psalm 78:5–6 says, "He commanded our fathers to teach their children, that the next generation might know them, the children yet unborn, and arise and tell them to their children."

- Proverbs 22:6 says, "Train up a child in the way he should go; even when he is old he will not depart from it."

- Luke 1:17 talks about God's prophet, giving him the task "to turn the hearts of the fathers to the children."

- Ephesians 6:4 commands us, "Fathers, do not provoke your children to anger, but bring them up in the discipline and instruction of the Lord."

- 1 Thessalonians 2:11–12 shows a picture of the relationship God wants us to have with our kids saying, "For you know how, like a father with his children, we exhorted each one of you and encouraged you and charged you to walk in a manner worthy of God."

- 1 Timothy 3:5 is part of a list of qualifications for leadership. It shows the importance of knowing how to care for your family before you can care for the church.

- 2 Timothy 1:5 and 3:15 speak of the faith that was passed down to Timothy from his mother, Eunice, and his grandmother, Lois. What an example and encouragement for those single-parent families and those where only mom has a heart for the Lord. God is still faithful!

Most parents, when they read these passages, feel the truth resonating in their hearts. Steve Farrar reminds us, "There is no 'new and improved' version to these commands. They have not been upgraded. They were perfect when they were given and they will be perfect for as long as men walk the earth. . . . The job description is timeless."[10] God has given you a great privilege. Your children are listening.

## APPARENT OPINIONS

We decided to put all the stats, studies, and biblical concepts to the test. In a survey we conducted of close to nine hundred students from sixteen different states,[11] we found what the experts found—students are listening.

- Ninety-eight percent of students surveyed wanted to pray with their parents as often or more often than they currently did.

- Ninety-seven percent of students wanted to read the Bible as often or more often than they currently did.

- Only 10 percent reported to read the Bible with their parents very often.

- When asked if they would follow their parents' advice, 41 percent said they would be very likely to and 54 percent somewhat likely. Only 5 percent would not be likely to follow their parents' advice.

We closed the survey with an open-ended question: "I wish my parents _____," asking students to fill in the blank. While one student wished his parents were superheroes, we were amazed with the profound answers we received. We saw the following answers over and over again:

I wish my parents . . .

- would take my Christianity seriously.
- would pray with me every night even when I'm getting ready to sleep.
- would start a family devotion.
- read the Bible with me more.
- helped me understand the Bible.
- would stay faithful to each other and God.
- would spend time together.
- would relate problems in life to Christian stories.
- would read the Bible with me more and pray with me more.
- did more things with the family.
- would stay the same forever.

We were shocked to see little or no talk of allowances, curfews, and friends. We saw close to a thousand times a desire from the young people for a family spiritual emphasis. Why? Because God wired our children to hunger for it. I challenge you to put our results to the test and try it yourself in your church. Others who have done so have found the same fact we have: young people are listening.

## They Are Listening

We cannot buy the lie any longer. God has given parents an incredible job assignment and responsibility. We have an apparent privilege without equal, every parent's privilege. Clearly our children are listening to us and we can influence them more than anyone else. Our children also listen to peers, and media, and teachers, but we don't need to be discouraged, unless we are remaining silent and letting others become the main influence. Our children are listening—no question about it.

I am concerned that we forget the privilege we have. We overlook the unparalleled influence of parenting. God has given us a place to affect our children for eternity. A personal hero of mine, John Angell James, a pastor from the mid-1800s, said, "Recollect what a solemn thing it is to be a parent, and what a weighty responsibility attaches to those who have the immortal souls of their children committed to their care!"[12] We cannot neglect the lasting things for the temporary. We cannot focus our efforts on passing things that the world says will offer soul satisfaction, or our children will find what Solomon found in Ecclesiastes as he discovered pursuing the things of the world is simply "striving after wind" (Ecclesiastes 1:17). We cannot help our children gain the whole world and yet forfeit their souls (Matthew 16:26). Your children are listening to you. You know the words of life they need to hear. Don't miss out on this apparent privilege of being a parent.

# A Parent's Voice: Why Your Children Need to Hear from You

Parents make the most ridiculous sounds to their newborns. It's like we lose our minds in an effort to connect with this tiny gift. I have seen the most rugged, tough, hard-as-pavement man's man pick up a small child and absolutely melt.

A few months ago, a former student from my ministry and her husband brought their newborn daughter to our house. Their daughter's name is Mecaden. I know we hear all the time about every baby being beautiful, but this one truly is dazzling. A few days after our families had lunch together they had a routine visit to the doctor where they discovered that their precious daughter had severe hearing loss. All of those songs, all of those compliments, all of those stories, all of those times they said, "I love you," and all of those prayers were never physically heard by Mecaden. Emily, Mecaden's mom, said it best: "I can remember the first time I heard the doctor say, 'Mrs. Bennett, your daughter has severe to profound hearing loss.' It was the most devastating thing I had ever heard in my life; something that screamed hopelessness and hurt into my soul."

Want some good news? What seemed to be so hopeless turned around in an instant. The fact that Mecaden had severe to profound hearing loss meant that she qualified for cochlear implants that she would not have qualified for if she had only moderate loss. Emily said, "God in His mercy has allowed Mecaden's hearing loss to be so profound that, as strange as it seems, she will hear us!" On the day before Mecaden's first birthday she heard her mom and dad say, "We love you. Mecaden, you are beautiful." The next day she heard her mom and dad sing, "Happy birthday." Her progress has continued to amaze mom, dad, and her doctors. They count as a blessing what other parents take for granted: a parent's privilege to simply speak to their children.

We must never underestimate the importance of our words. Paul David Tripp said, "Words are powerful, important, significant. When we speak, it must be with the realization that God has given our words significance. God has given our words value."[13] There are four primary reasons why our children need to hear us.

**Words share the good news.** You have the privilege to tell your children the most important news they will ever hear: that Jesus Christ loves them, and died to save them from their sins. Romans 10:17 says, "Faith comes from hearing, and hearing through the word of Christ." You have the opportunity to share daily the most important message with your children through your words and actions. This message of the Gospel is crucial for them in coming to know Christ personally, but the Gospel also is important in their daily walk with Christ. Every day we must remember that we are sinners saved by the grace of God who sent His Son to die for us. If the cross of Christ is the center of history, then it must also be the center of our lives as well as the center of our communication with our children. There simply is no better use of your words to your children than bringing eternal truths to bear in your daily interactions with your child.

**Words communicate love.** Your words speak to your children's souls. They say, "I love you" and "I value you so much that I will spend time with you in conversation." Proverbs 16:24 says, "Gracious words are like a honeycomb, sweetness to the soul and health to the body." Your words communicate love to your child.

**Words have weight.** There are words and then there are *words*. No parent truly realizes the weight of their words to their children. How many grown men struggle for decades simply because a parent never said, "Son, I love you"? Our words—or the lack of them—are heavy. It has been said that the vast majority of inmates were told as children, "One day you will end up in prison." This is why Solomon warned in Proverbs 12:18: "There is one whose rash words are like sword thrusts, but the tongue of the wise brings healing." Wise parents understand the weight of their words.

**Words affect the heart.** Words from a parent not only set the course of life but also can be used by God to affect eternity. Proverbs 4:20 says, "My son, be attentive to my words; incline your ear to my sayings." Your kids are listening and they need to hear from you. They need you to speak up. Ephesians 4:29 says that our words can "give grace to those who hear." Your words can be a means of grace to your children, point them to where God is working in their lives, and help shape their lives and destiny.

## THE REALITY OUR KIDS FACE

If there is one group I identify with, it is parents— I understand the unique challenges we all face. I have served in student ministry for more than twenty years. My profession affords me the wonderful opportunity to meet with parents almost on a daily basis, not to mention the fact that I have three children of my own. All of this has caused me to become an advocate for parents. Because I am around parents so much, I can say with 100 percent certainty that parents today are anxious. The vast majority of parents I meet seek to grow and aspire to become better parents. They genuinely desire to have children who place their full hope in Christ alone.

We aren't the first to feel this burden. Even Solomon with all of his wisdom shared our concern, beginning his writings to his sons saying, "Hear, my son, your father's instruction" (Proverbs 1:8). As a dad, I can imagine Solomon's concern about all the challenges life would throw his children's way as he wrote his book of wisdom.

Would you assume that we have more concerns than Solomon did in his day? I would. Have the advancements of civilization, government, education, and economy helped us create safer environments for our children? They have not. Most parents I know are very concerned about the dangers and challenges our children face in this culture. Our children face an even greater danger against an enemy who seeks to "steal and kill and destroy" (John 10:10).

There are four major shifts in our culture that intensify the struggles our children face; four culture shifts we must be aware of as we build up and protect our children.

### 1. Shifting battleground

I can't speak for you, but my childhood home was (for the most part) a safe, stable place I enjoyed. Today, some of our children's homes are no longer places of retreat. What families used to keep at arm's length from their children, the media brings right into our own homes every day. What Solomon warned his son to avoid as he walked down the street is now just a remote or mouse click away. This current battle bombards our kids with sexed-up media, Internet pornography, and increasingly graphic violence. Here's how the battle has shifted into new arenas:

- The average age for first exposure to pornography is twelve. Eighty-eight percent of teens have been exposed to pornography.[14]

- Do an Internet search sometime on "How to kill your-self." The most recent search I did found 5,370,000 pages, including pages on "Cool ways to kill yourself" and ways to kill yourself that most hurt your parents.[15]

- Children ages thirteen to fifteen on average see three hours of TV per day, which contains more sexual content than ever before.[16]

- Nearly two out of three TV shows contained some form of violence. Even the average child who watches two hours of cartoons a day may see ten thousand acts of violence in a year.[17]

- Even our video games have changed. "Donkey Kong" and "Space Invaders" have evolved into games like "Playboy the Mansion" and "Grand Theft Auto," programmed with hidden sex scenes.[18]

Children need their moms and dads to fight to keep this battle outside the walls of their home. Steve Farrar says, "The greatest sin our sons will face in their life is sexual sins because he is a man and because of the time in which we live."[19] We all, especially young people, need a safe haven. It is our job as parents to be protectors of our children. We must be willing to do whatever it takes to protect and defend the gift God has given us. This commitment is seen clearly in John 15:13: "Greater love has no one than this, that someone lay down his life for his friends." This is the kind of commitment that defends and protects our kids.

## 2. Shifting morals

A generation ago, many of those with strong morals were admired. Today they are bullied, teased, and despised. A generation ago conservative, Bible-believing Christians were considered the salt of the earth. Today they are considered bigots and intolerant. Imagine making a stand in almost any of our universities today, stating that homosexuality goes against God's created order. You'd be labeled narrow-minded, treated as an extremist, and accused of hate speech. One school in our region does not permit students to form a Christian club, but offers one for alternative lifestyles instead. The morals of today have definitely shifted.

What once was clearly defined as right and wrong is no longer as clear today. Our culture no longer embraces absolute truth; rather it is viewed as optional, up for debate, and based on personal interpretation. Our culture reasons that something can be true for one person, but not for another. Morals are no longer consistent. Family values depend on what family you ask. Here's a peek into the reality our children face:

• David Kinnaman, vice president of one of the largest Christian research organizations, writes that moral decisions for today's generation are most often made by whatever feels comfortable or whatever causes the least amount of conflict.[20]

- He also writes, "In virtually every study we conduct, representing thousands of interviews every year, born-again Christians fail to display much attitudinal or behavioral evidence of transformed lives. Most of the lifestyle activities of born-again Christians are statistically equivalent to those of non-born-agains. When asked to identify their activities over the last thirty days, born-again believers were just as likely to bet or gamble, to visit a pornographic web site, to take something that did not belong to them, to consult a medium or psychic, to physically fight or abuse someone, to have consumed enough alcohol to be considered legally drunk, to have used illegal, nonprescription drug, or to have said something about someone that was not true. . . . No difference."[21]

- Baby boomers self-reported that the main goals for life are a good family life and a good marriage.[22] This generation of young people self-reports that their main goals are personal fame and wealth.[23]

- Premarital sex is now accepted as everyday behavior, and is now widely prevalent among young people. The Centers for Disease Control has released its numbers of sex and teens.

PERCENTAGE WHO HAVE HAD INTERCOURSE:

| AGE GROUP | % OF BOYS | % OF GIRLS |
|---|---|---|
| Before age 13 | 9 | 4 |
| 9th grade | 39 | 29 |
| 10th grade | 42 | 44 |
| 11th grade | 51 | 52 |
| 12th grade | 64 | 62 |

Source: Centers for Disease Control and Prevention (2006)

• We have record numbers of sexually transmitted diseases, especially chlamydia, according to the CDC.[24]

• A Gallup Poll determined that the majority of Americans believe divorce, gambling, and premarital sex "pass the test of moral acceptability." [25]

What clearly used to be wrong is now up for debate in the culture, but it shouldn't be up for debate in Christian homes. Children need moms and dads who refuse to compromise God-given truths. We cannot allow biblical standards of right and wrong to erode under the pressure of a feel-good society. This society listens to the lies of "Boys will be boys" and "Just let your children sow their wild oats." It is scary to see parents assume that times have changed so much that they must allow their kids to participate in behaviors that are dangerous, unwise, or clearly sinful. While times may change, God's standards have not.

Our children need us to help define lines that are becoming blurrier by the minute.

Paul warns Timothy about the last days. He says, "People will be lovers of self, lovers of money, proud, arrogant, abusive, disobedient to their parents, ungrateful, unholy... and will turn away from listening to the truth and wander off into myths" (2 Timothy 3:2; 4:4). Sound familiar? We cannot allow our kids to navigate this shifting moral landscape alone. We must stay close to them to help them determine right from wrong. *USA Today* echoes this advice: "You have to remain close to your kids. . . . You can't just say, 'They're teenagers, they're obnoxious. I'm checking out, and I'll see them again at 20.' Warmth from parents and clear, firm guidelines can make a big difference to kids this age."[26] Parents who address this shifting of morals, instead of running from the facts, will best serve Christ and their families.

### 3. Shifting to a post-Christian nation

Many experts believe that America is now a post-Christian nation. While our nation was founded to be a society of religious freedom, it seems that Christianity is not free to express itself any longer. Sunday mornings are no longer sacred, but are now prime time for sports leagues and extracurricular activities. Prayer before a football game or at graduation is no longer prayer "in Jesus name" or to our "Heavenly Father," but rather to the "god of many names" and "unknowable One." Passing out condoms at school is politically correct, but passing out a flyer about a Christian event is proselytizing and not allowed. America is not the Christian nation it once was, and our children are now facing pressure and persecution that we never faced. Here are the facts:

- The U.S. has always been a majority Protestant nation, but no longer. The number of Americans who claim to be affiliated with Protestant denominations will soon be a minority percentage. In contrast, as recently as the mid-1980s, surveys found that approximately two-thirds of the population was Protestant.[27]

- Among Americans ages eighteen to twenty-nine, one in four say they are not currently affiliated with a particular religion.[28]

- After the most impressive research of his day, Thom Rainer, Christian researcher and author, stated that if current trends continue, only 4 percent of this generation of young people will stand for Christ.[29]

- A recent nationwide survey completed by the Barna Research Group determined that only 4 percent of Americans had a biblical worldview.[30]

- Christianity is no longer the main religion and is declining in many places. In England, for example, the most common name for newborn males is no longer George or Jack; it is now Mohammed.[31]

- David Kinnaman writes about the hatred toward Bible-believing Christians: "We discovered that outsiders expressed the most opposition toward evangelicals... the views are extraordinarily negative. Disdain for evangelicals is overwhelming and definitive."[32]

Growing up in the Bible Belt, I felt like everyone around me seemingly held the same Christian values. That is no longer true today. We have to equip our children with tools that we didn't have to use. They must be able to identify and understand the different worldviews out there but also be able to articulate a biblical worldview. They must be on guard and constantly filtering the messages they are receiving and understanding that most of the messages from the culture are in direct opposition to the Word of God. In short, our kids have to understand what they believe and how it is different than what others around them believe.

### 4. Shifting adolescences

When you turn eighteen, you become an adult, right? Not so fast. Today, the line between child and adult is harder to find. Now there is a gap between childhood and adulthood that lasts for many years and causes many new problems. Here are the facts:

- Teenagers are new inventions. In most of history (and still in other cultures today), once a person hit puberty, he or she was no longer a child but was considered to be an adult. Until the 1950s, the word *teenager* wasn't used and was never in a dictionary.[33]

- One cultural researcher said that the teen years were invented to become a second childhood. It was created because of cultural changes as America became more urban and industrialized.[34]

- Christian Smith, researcher of the largest study ever conducted on the beliefs of young people, writes, "Between 1950 and 2000, the median age of first marriage for women rose from 20 to 25 years old. For men during that same time the median age rose from 22 to 27 years old. The sharpest increase for both took place after 1970. Half a century ago, many young people were anxious to get out of high school, marry, settle down, have children and start a long-term career. But many youth today, especially but not exclusively men, face almost a decade between high school graduation and marriage to spend exploring life's many options in unprecedented freedom."[35]

- Smith also correctly points out what emotions accompany this lengthening of youth: "(1) identity exploration, (2) instability, (3) focus on self, (4) feeling in limbo, in transition, in-between, and (5) sense of possibilities, opportunities and unparalleled hope. These, of course, are also often accompanied by big doses of transience, confusion, anxiety, self-obsession, melodrama, conflict, and disappointment."[36]

- *Money Magazine* writes, "Boomerang kids are now so common that social scientists have dubbed the phenomenon 'adultolescence,' a period following college that can last five or more years. More than 65 percent of graduates are moving back home, compared with 53 percent just five years ago. And while the difficult stages of childhood may have had lasting emotional impact, this one has financial ramifications galore for you—about $5,000 a year, on average, in assistance—and your kid."[37]

- Young people are also not as interested in starting a family. David Kinnaman says, "Many young people do not expect to be married or to begin a family as a young adult (or at all), though this may have been the expectation in the past."[38]

Our children need mothers and fathers to help them become adults. Childhood is temporary. One goal of parenting is to lay the groundwork to help children become godly adults. We must continually show our children what it means to be a biblical woman and a biblical man. We must teach responsibility, respect, work ethic, spiritual maturity, and life skills that adults must have. Paul said, "When I was a child, I spoke like a child, I thought like a child, I reasoned like a child. When I became a man, I gave up childish ways" (1 Corinthians 13:11). We must help our children learn the difference between childhood and adulthood.

Parents should protect their children and provide the guidance needed to traverse through the minefields of life. Kids need you, mom and dad. Speak up. Fight for them. Never give up. They are counting on us.

## GREAT NEWS!

God has placed you and me in our children's corner, fighting for them, praying for them, modeling for them, protecting them, nurturing them, and picking them up when they fall. They have us as a daily mentor—the primary spiritual discipler.

You may feel unprepared, ill equipped, not cool enough, or that you don't know the Scripture well enough. Do you see any reasons you aren't qualified for the task God has called you to? If so, you are in good company. Abraham was too old. Jeremiah was too young. Solomon was too rich. Jesus was too poor. Paul was a murderer. Moses was a murderer. Jonah ran from God. Elijah got depressed and was suicidal. Martha worried too much. Gideon and Thomas doubted. David had an affair. When we are weak, He is strong. You may feel that someone else would do a better job—maybe a youth pastor or your child's Bible study teacher. This logic will not work, and today's statistics and research prove that parents are primary to teaching the Gospel of Christ to their children. You are God's main plan, His "A-Team," and you must take hold of this role that God has laid squarely at your feet and perfectly equipped you to do. God gave us our specific children for a reason, and He never gives us a task that He will not help us perform. His grace is sufficient!

The Scriptures make it very apparent that parents, especially fathers, are assigned the role of teaching their children this incredible Gospel.

- Exodus 13:8 and following says that we must tell our children what the Lord has done for us.

- God commands us to teach His commandments "to your children and your children's children" (Deuteronomy 4:9).

- Some of the last words Moses wrote were: "Take to heart all the words by which I am warning you today, that you may command them to your children, that they may be careful to do all the words of this law. For it is no empty word for you, but your very life" (Deuteronomy 32:46–47).

- Proverbs 1:8–9 says, "Hear, my son, your father's instruction, and forsake not your mother's teaching, for they are a graceful garland for your head and pendants for your neck."

- The prophet Isaiah tells us, "The father makes known to the children your faithfulness" (Isaiah 38:19).

- In the New Testament, we discover that the youthful pastor Timothy had been faithfully taught the Holy Scriptures from childhood (2 Timothy 3:15).

• Paul writes, "Children obey your parents in everything, for this pleases the Lord. Fathers, do not provoke your children, lest they become discouraged" (Colossians 3:20–21).

One of today's leading Christian researchers says, "Responsibility for raising spiritual champions, according to the Bible, belongs to parents. The spiritual nurture of children is supposed to be done in the home. Organizations and people from outside the home might support those efforts, but the responsibility is squarely laid at the feet of the family." [39]

The Search Institute, another leading research organization, states, "People seem to intuitively 'know' that parents have an impact on children. For the most part, research supports what people already know: parents are, indeed, the largest influence on how children think, feel, and act."[40]

Ed Gamble, who now leads the Southern Baptist Association of Christian Schools, said, "Historically, professional educators are the pros. But, God did not give professional educators children. He gave children to parents and they are the ones whom God holds accountable for the way their children turn out."[41]

It is unanimous. The Bible says that parents are primary. Research says that parents are primary. Experience and common sense both say that parents are primary. Do we truly believe it?

You may feel anxious because of the shifting ground surrounding your family. You may be overwhelmed when you hear about the power of your words. You may think that parenting your children is your biggest problem right now, but let me remind you that God has already taken care of your biggest problem—sin and separation from a holy God. Your reconciliation to God will give you much hope when facing the challenges of parenting. If you are a believer in Christ, remember we have this great hope, and we have God to help us. "He who began a good work in you will bring it to completion at the day of Christ Jesus" (Philippians 1:6). "Your Father knows what you need before you ask him" (Matthew 6:8). God has already taken care of our biggest problem; and He will strengthen you, give you hope, and supply your strength as you speak eternal words of life into your children's souls.

# A PARENT'S UNDERSTANDING: A THEOLOGY OF FAMILY

In 1999, an earthquake in Izmit, Turkey, tragically killed upward of fifty thousand people.[42] The scope of this disaster is tough to even get your mind around. It leaves you asking questions like "Why?" The Turkish government sought out an independent agency to analyze what went wrong, and their researchers found several contributing factors:

- Most of the buildings in the area did not meet the design requirements and so were not built to withstand a catastrophe.
- Building contractors routinely ignored earthquake specifications.
- Most of the buildings were built with inappropriate materials and poor workmanship.
- Many buildings were knowingly built on active fault lines and in high-risk areas.
- Many buildings were not designed by experts, but built according to what others were doing.[43]

Could the same things be said about many of today's families?

- Do most of our families meet God's design requirements, preparing them to withstand the storms of life?
- How closely have most of our families followed God's specifications from His Word?
- Are our families built on lasting principles or with poor materials such as passing trends and shifting opinions?
- Why are many Christian families knowingly built with high-risk indicators being ignored, causing a divorce epidemic in the church?
- How many families are built on God's Word, rather than on simply what others are doing?

In Matthew 7:24–28, Jesus taught this familiar parable:

> Everyone then who hears these words of mine and does them will be like a wise man who built his house on the rock. And the rain fell, and the floods came, and the winds blew and beat on that house, but it did not fall, because it had been founded on the rock. And everyone who hears these words of mine and does not do them will be like a foolish man who built his house on the sand. And the rain fell, and the floods came, and the winds blew and beat against that house, and it fell, and great was the fall of it.
> And when Jesus finished these sayings, the crowds were

astonished at His teaching.

There are difficult times in life that reveal the strength of our foundations. Much could be said about the erosion of the family we see today. Many are ignoring God's design for the family, and we are all seeing the effects: the divorce epidemic, teen STDs at record numbers, the beginnings of a fatherless nation, and so on. Like you, I don't want these things in my family. I want my home to stand strong through whatever storms of life come our way. Better yet, God wants our homes to stand strong. We see in Romans 12:2 that God's will for all of us is "good and acceptable and perfect." Did you catch that? God has a good, acceptable, perfect will for our families. This simple truth has radically changed my perspective on Christian parenting. It provides great confidence for Tina and me as we realize that God has a role for us to play in our partnership with Him. God's vision for us and our children is that He will raise them to be who He created them to be in order to receive glory through their lives, even through the storms of life.

I'm afraid that we may be so familiar with family that we never stop to think about what it is supposed to look like. All of us are in a family at some point or in some way during our lives; wouldn't it make sense to have a "theology of family"? That phrase may sound a bit overwhelming to you. When I mentioned it to a friend of mine, Dr. Allen Jackson, professor at New Orleans Baptist Theological Seminary, he broke it down for me. He said that "theology" is thinking about God. So a "theology of family" would be "thinking about how God thinks about family." That's a great, yet simple, explanation—and a great goal for this chapter.

Not long ago I walked outside our house and immediately smelled smoke. After I checked everything around the house, I decided the smoke must have been coming from somewhere else. As I left my house, the smoke only got worse, and there was thick smoke everywhere. Raleigh was covered in a blanket that looked like one huge cloud. Visibility was only a half mile. The news report on the radio said that the smoke was a result of a fire 120 miles away that started a month earlier. I remembered hearing reports about the fire for weeks, but on that particular day, the winds had turned just right and smoke from the fire hit home. Everywhere you went everyone was talking about it. We all had known about it for a while, but it was far away and something we never thought about. That taught me a lesson—until danger hits home, it doesn't feel real to us.

Most of us can think of dozens of sermons, news reports, and other warnings we've received about the dangers that surround our families. However, many of us ignore the smoke until it hits home as we discover pornography on our computer, or our daughter tells us she is pregnant, or we realize our child is drifting from God. As stated earlier, the institution of the family is under attack. Following are real-life questions your children are being bombarded with daily.

- "Why would we need to get married? Why not just live together?" That is what others are doing, since marriage rates are down 20 percent over the past decade.[44] One newspaper even reported that "marriage may no longer be the perfect union" since marriage rates continue to fall and divorce is at an all-time high.[45]

- "Why would we want to have kids? Won't they interfere with my life's goals?" There is a new demographic called "childless by choice," which includes 4.1 million women who do not want children.[46] This trend made headlines when a British paper reported on a woman who felt it was wrong to have children because it hurts the environment. She said, 'Having children is selfish. It's all about maintaining your genetic line at the expense of the planet."[47]

- "Who is marriage for—men and women, or whoever wants to be called married?" This is headline news in Massachusetts and California, as they are beginning to allow same-sex unions.[48] Not surprisingly, we are now seeing our first gay divorces.[49]

- "Can we walk away from family when it is no longer convenient for our lifestyle?" We all know about the 50 percent divorce rates for first-time marriages, but the rates are 67 percent for second marriages and 74 percent for third marriages.[50] Researchers are suggesting that people are accepting the idea of serial marriages, lasting a few years until it is time to find a partner who better fits their current lifestyle.[51]

• "What are the roles within the family? Is there a difference between men and women?" Oakland Elementary School makes no distinction between boys and girls, letting boys play girls in skits and vice versa. They have unisex restrooms and have thrown out the idea of gender for young children[52] In marriage, we now see the lines more blurred than ever before.[53]

You know these issues are on the front burner of society, and unless we clearly communicate our theology to our children many of them will be swept away in an avalanche of public opinion. Where do our children go for answers? Oprah? Dr. Phil? Planned Parenthood? Government agencies? Celebrities? The Internet? Who will define what marriage and family is for our children?

God does not change. His Word does not fluctuate with the times. His truths that guide our families are enduring, unshakable, and trustworthy. We need to think about family, like God thinks about family. We need a theology of family.

## THEOLOGY OF FAMILY

Why is a correct understanding of family so important? Ephesians 5 is a good place to find an answer to that question. Notice closely, Paul continually compares the relationship between husband and wife to the relationship between Christ and the church. He talks about how a husband and wife become one flesh and says, "I am saying that it refers to Christ and the church" (Ephesians 5:32). I can't imagine Paul laboring over the right image to explain family relationships. "It's like the sun and moon . . . no . . . It's like how the ground needs rain . . . no . . . I know . . . It's like Christ and the church." I'm being sarcastic to make a point. It wasn't like Paul was racking his brain for an analogy to describe family. The Bible always describes family relationships and our relationship with God in the same terms. God is the Father. Christ is His Son. We are His children. The church is His Bride. When God talked about the sin of His people to Hosea, what image did He use? Adultery. Song of Solomon is full of images that relate to marital love and love for God. In Hebrews 12:7–11, when He talks about His sanctifying work in our lives, He talks about fatherly discipline. Heaven is referred to as a "marriage supper" in Revelation 19:9. Salvation is portrayed as "adoption" in Romans 8:15. Family language is used all throughout the Bible.

Here's the point: God designed marriage and family to represent and mirror a covenant relationship between God and us. To sum up this great passage on marriage in Ephesians 5, Paul says that the entire time he was talking about Christ and the church. He's not changing gears between two subjects; there is one subject—the Gospel is represented in Christian marriage. This passage isn't about healthier marriages, but about theology (thinking about God) and ecclesiology (thinking about the church). Christian marriage makes a strong statement about the Gospel to our kids, our spouses, and the world. A theology of Christian marriage and family is crucial because it is shows the many facets of Christ's love, such as selflessness, sacrifice, forgiveness, purity, and grace.

Divorce is a tragedy on numerous levels, but the primary heartbreak of divorce is that it doesn't reflect the truth of God's love. His love is unfailing, unselfish, and unending in its commitment to His Bride. He gave marriage and family to reflect His character and portray the Gospel in everyday life. That is why family and our understanding of it is of utmost importance. Our understanding of family cannot be separated from our understanding of God and the Gospel.[54]

## SEVEN FOUNDATIONS OF THE THEOLOGY OF FAMILY

God does not hide the way we should think about family in the fine print of the Bible. It is clearly laid out in many of the passages you and I know by heart. Here are seven foundations—seven bedrock truths God gives us in His Word that will stand strong through all of life's storms:

**FOUNDATION 1. God created man and woman in His image.** Genesis 1:27 says, "God created man in his own image, in the image of God he created him, male and female he created them." God created each gender with intentional and specific characteristics. Dr. Randy Stinson, executive director of the Council for Biblical Manhood and Womanhood, says it well:

Roles between men and women originated in the pre-fall garden and subsequently apply to all human beings.

Since roles are a part of the original creation, then they are inherent in the lives of all men and women and thus should find an echo in every human heart. The idea that men and women are equal yet different, though rejected by modern feminism, is indeed a result of God's purposeful and beautiful design.[55]

**FOUNDATION 2. God blessed man and woman with the gifts of marriage, sex, and family.** Genesis 1:28 records God telling the first family to "be fruitful and multiply and fill the earth." Also Genesis 2:24 gives foundational principles for families: "Therefore a man shall leave his father and his mother and hold fast to his wife, and they shall become one flesh." The definition of marriage is now a hot debate, with some states no longer issuing marriage licenses for brides and grooms, but now "Party A" and "Party B," whichever gender they choose.[56] Not so in the Bible. God's design is to join man and woman together. He created the first family. Family didn't evolve from societal needs for financial stability and domestic support. God created family, just as He created man and woman. Sex was created as a gift from God to bring a husband and wife closer together for enjoyment and to procreate a family. Countless problems arise in our society when people try to separate sex from God's design of marriage: fatherless societies, STDs, promiscuity, sexual addictions, molestation, homosexuality, abuses, pornography, and so on. However, when Christian marriage functions as God intended, men and women are fulfilled in their roles and children are brought into a loving family where they will hear the Word of God taught and watch the Gospel on display.

**FOUNDATION 3. God gave parents the primary role of spiritually discipling their children.** In years of teaching on this subject, I always begin by asking the same question: "As you open up God's Word, who do you find that God has put in place to be the primary discipler of children?" In all of the years of asking this question, no one has ever missed the answer. God gave parents the primary discipleship role. The peak of this teaching is called the Shema and is found in Deuteronomy 6:4–9:

> Hear, O Israel: The LORD our God, the LORD is one. You shall love the LORD your God with all your heart and with all your soul and with all your might. And these words that I command you today shall be on your heart. You shall teach them diligently to your children, and shall talk of them when you sit in your house, and when you walk by the way, and when you lie down, and when you rise. You shall bind them as a sign on your hand, and they shall be as frontlets between your eyes. You shall write them on the doorposts of your house and on your gates.

This isn't just a Jewish or Old Testament principle. It is also found in Ephesians 6:4, saying, "Fathers, do not provoke your children to anger, but bring them up in the discipline and instruction of the Lord." Before there were churches, Sunday schools, and youth groups, God entrusted parents with the privilege to teach their children. This command hasn't changed. There is no Shema Version 2.0. Teaching our children about the Lord is our privilege and responsibility as parents. John Angell James said,

Here fix your center; here direct your aim; here concentrate your efforts, your energies, and your prayers. Remember, their religious education is your business. Whatever aids you call in from ministers or teachers, you never must, you never can, you never should, delegate this work. God will hold you responsible for the religion of your children.[57]

**FOUNDATION 4. God calls husbands to love their wives and calls wives to submit to their husbands.** Ephesians 5, as we have seen, is the foundational passage on this topic. Verse 22 says, "Wives, submit to your own husbands, as to the Lord." Just as God created family, He did so with an order to it. The Bible is clear that God sees husbands as the head of a family, regardless of what is popular in today's culture. A husband has the privilege, responsibility, and duty to lovingly lead his family. Verses 25–26 clarify this, saying, "Husbands, love your wives, as Christ loved the church and gave himself up for her, that he might sanctify her, having cleansed her by the washing of water with the word." Husbands must remember that Christ Himself modeled the kind of leadership they are instructed to provide when He willingly laid down His life to honor His Bride. Christ's love was selfless. Christ's example should compel husbands to out-serve and cherish their wives.

**FOUNDATION 5. God's design is for marriage to be lifelong**. God hates divorce. That may sound harsh, but I didn't say it; God did in Malachi 2:16 (NIV): "I hate divorce." The Bible is unified in its teaching against divorce. Unfortunately churches have been growing silent in regards to this teaching. Christian marriage is sacred, as it represents Christ's commitment to His Bride. Ephesians 5:28, which tells husbands to love their wives "in the same way" Christ loves us, reminds us that our marriage commitment speaks to the world that Christ's love for His Bride is enduring.

I am not saying that divorce is an unforgivable sin or that divorcees can never serve Christ. What I am saying is that God's design is clear. His framework is for marriage to last. He wants our marriages to be light in the world, and churches must do all it can to rescue marriages caught in the storms of life.

**FOUNDATION 6. God seeks to use Christian families as a testimony of His love for His children.** Second Corinthians 5:20 is a compelling passage that tells us, "Therefore, we are ambassadors for Christ, God making his appeal through us." Our families must be representatives to the world on God's behalf.

What makes your family different than every other family on the block? Is there something more than the fact that you go to church? Our families must be distinct from those of the world, serving as a very real picture of Christ's love for us.

Do we see our marriages as a Gospel presentation? We should. It shows the Gospel to everyone around us. How is our marriage different than a Buddhist marriage or Muslim marriage? The presence of Christ in our marriage must drastically change it. Christian marriages should be marked with confessing sin, asking forgiveness, serving selflessly and in humility regarding your partner as "more significant than yourselves" (Philippians 2:3). Christ is making His appeal to the world through our marriage and our family, so the way we understand family is extremely important.

**FOUNDATION 7. God's design is for families to unite and partner with the local church for the mutual purpose of discipleship.** In Genesis, God created the first institution—the family. He creates the second institution in the New Testament—the church. So how are we to view these two institutions? Are they rivals? Is one no longer needed? I believe the Bible teaches that the church and family are to be united for the same purpose. Deuteronomy 6:7 says that families are to "diligently teach [God's Word] to your children," but God says the same thing of the church in Ephesians 4:12, giving the church the task to "equip the saints." Families are to teach young people. Churches are to teach all people, including young people. Why the overlap? Because the church and the family are to be united to accomplish discipleship. Families should no more drop their kids off at the church door to be discipled any more than they should avoid the church and try to go it alone. Family and church need each other to function like each is designed to function for the glory of God.

## Passing It Down

You may think these foundations sound familiar and are overly simple. You may have heard them all before, but how clearly can you articulate a theology of family? Even more crucial, does your family reflect what you say you believe? Are these bedrock principles in your life and the recurring theme in your conversations with your kids? Test yourself. Ask your children, "What are the biblical foundations for family that God has put in place?" How many of the seven will they know? You may be shocked like I was when a girl in my church said, "The best Christians at my school are the homosexuals." Times have changed, and that is why a clearly stated theology of family is crucial.

I grew up on Ponderosa Lane in a small town in north Georgia. The people who lived on my road included Betty Sue, Harold Dean, Henrietta, Ruth, and Blondeen. I remember their names because they are my aunts and uncles, and they all had the same basic Christian worldview. If I went over to their home for dinner and saw something on the news, they would tell me what God thought about that topic. Then I'd go to play with a cousin and hear the same thing and later go home and hear the same thing. Not so today. Talk radio says one thing, the cable news show says another, the Internet blogger says another, the ball coach says another, the Mormon neighbor says another, and the university professor says another. We can't assume that our children will pick up a clear understanding of Christian family just by growing older. We must take hold of the privilege to share a theology of family with our children. They need to hear from us first because they are already hearing from so many others.

## BUILT TO LAST

The storms of life will come. Jesus promised that it rains on the "just and on the unjust" (Matthew 5:45). Is there anyone you know who hasn't dealt with the loss of a job, a loved one, their savings, a child, their health, or something else? I don't know anyone who has escaped all storms of life. The question isn't, "Will the storms of life come?" The question is, "Will I be prepared when they do?"

A couple of years ago, my family was hit with two of the biggest storms we have ever faced, both within a two-month period. These storms involved betrayals, broken hearts, and late nights of tearful conversations. Honestly, the hardship and residue from these storms will last for years to come. As we felt our children were mature enough, we shared pieces of the struggles with them. They knew that mom and dad were going through a storm in life, and they watched how we handled it. We hoped to model dependency on God and hoped our children saw that we were not sovereign, but God is. We learned about prayer together and our grasp of theology was strengthened. When these storms laid bare our foundation, I learned that His grace is sufficient. When the storms came, we didn't run to motivational speakers or some book we found in the self-help section, but we turned to God and He saw us through. We saw the promises of God's Word come to life. God really was our "refuge and strength, a very present help in trouble" (Psalm 46:1).

Quite honestly, we all practice theology every day. Theology isn't head knowledge for pastors. It is what affects our everyday lives and what we hold on to through the storms of life. Just as the parable stated, you and I are building our homes on a foundation. Are we building our homes on a storm-proof foundation that only Christ provides? These storms reveal why it is crucial to understand a theology of family: thinking about how God thinks about family.

# A Parent's Difference: Why the Difference Should Be Apparent

It has been said that the game of golf is much like the game of life—it's a lot easier to talk about than to do. There are innumerable obstacles, entrapments, and challenges that test one's mettle. William, my middle child, is learning these facts firsthand. He is naturally gifted as a golfer, and last year he made the high school golf team as a seventh grader. William is small for his age, which is magnified as he often plays against guys twice his size. On the first tee box, he says the key is to control his nerves when he sees all the giants surrounding him. He has the perfect demeanor for golf. He almost never loses his cool—he displays a calm and steadiness no matter what happens on the course. When something goes wrong his response is, "This is what I practiced for all those hours. I'm ready for this."

As any competitive golfer can tell you, the climax of every match is the walk to the eighteenth green. As William approaches the finish, the crowd is there; everyone he loves is there cheering for him. I am always watching to see how he finishes. You don't even have to see the scorecards, because how these young golfers fared is written clearly on their faces. Even on the PGA Tour, you can tell the importance of this moment even to those men who have made that walk thousands of times. Some finish proud. Others hang their heads in disappointment.

As I said, the game of golf is a lot like the game of life. We can focus on the traps out there. We can panic after each mistake we make. Or we can remember that the goal of it all is finishing well. Many parents today get bogged down in the craze of the day, forgetting they only have twelve or nine or two more holes to play . . . or maybe less. Sure, the issues we face today are very real and often can make us panic for a moment, but the goal of Christian parenting isn't to simply avoid today's trouble. Biblical parenting is more than keeping our kids from having sex, using drugs, or going to jail. It is about fostering an awe of God in our children. It is about showing our children their need for a Savior and introducing them to Jesus who alone can rescue their lives from sin and give life that lasts forever.

I am often inspired as I see William make his walk after eighteen holes of golf. I hope I can finish as well after eighteen years of parenting. As I cheer for him, I think of Hebrews 12:1 that says we, too, are surrounded by a cloud of witnesses cheering us on. As a parent, I want nothing more than to finish well. I know you feel the same.

So, are you and I prepared for the task at hand? Do we have a clear understanding of the biblical principles that should guide us as Christian parents? God's Word has much to say about this topic, and the vast majority of parents I meet desperately want to be guided by biblical principles that will help them raise children who are passionate for Christ. Let's examine some biblical principles that apply to toddlers and teens, wayward kids and those who beg to go to church. The Bible has something to say for every situation, every child, and every parent.

There are several distinctive marks of Christian parents clearly found in the pages of Scripture, which change the way we raise our children.

## What Makes Biblical Parenting Unique?

Christian parenting is often misunderstood. Some people think there is an easy five-step program to picture-perfect kids in five easy weeks. The Bible doesn't paint this concept of parenting at all. It speaks of prodigals. It tells us about the brokenhearted. It deals straightforwardly with communication problems and anger. It never says that parenting is simple and never promises perfect kids. Christian parenting is anything but easy. However, God's Word spells out how we can make the best of every situation.

Christian parenting comes in all shapes and sizes. Some parents think their children are "perfect" because they would rather spend Fridays at a Bible study than at a party with friends. On the other hand, there are parents who do everything to provide an environment that is Christ-centered and loving, and their children still test them at every turn. There are cultural distinctions, economic differences, and educational preferences. Now, more than any time before, there are blended, single-parent, and nontraditional families that add new challenges to what was already a challenging endeavor. Can one book speak to all of these situations? I believe the Bible can. The Bible never promises an easy path, but it gives us principles that anyone can incorporate, and it promises that God will give us strength. Our situations constantly change, but there is hope in the one truth that never changes—God's Word!

So, what is Christian parenting? How is it different than non-Christian parenting? How is "good" parenting different than godly parenting? Sadly today these are tougher questions to answer for many. There are many families attending church weekly who aren't practicing Christian parenting. They believe that the primary task of Christian parenting is taking your kids to church for a couple hours a week. Nothing could be more wrong. Christian parenting affects every day, not just Sundays. It has a different motive, a different goal, and—good Lord willing—a different outcome.

Here are four distinctive marks of Christian parenting:

- Christian parents seek to model the Gospel.
- Christian parents value and protect the sanctity of Christian marriage.
- Christian parents see their children as blessings.
- Christian parents desire that Jesus captivate their children's hearts.

## 1. Christian parents seek to model the Gospel.

We are Christ-followers who seek to model what it means to live the Gospel daily before our children. Christian parenting is not "Do as I say, not as I do." We strive to be the best models for our kids so they might see us aware of our need for God, living repentant lives, striving to trust God fully and being authentic. Understand that we are not perfect models—only Christ bears that distinction. The Bible doesn't require us to be perfect parents. Instead, we can model grace after failure, forgiveness after sin, and restoration after disagreements. In tremendous success and in utter failure, we must understand the impact of modeling the Gospel for the little eyes daily watching us. Paul's statement could be a mission statement for parenting: "Be imitators of me, as I am of Christ" (1 Corinthians 11:1). In another letter he says something very similar: "Show yourself in all respects to be a model of good works, and in your teaching show integrity, dignity, and sound speech that cannot be condemned" (Titus 2:7–8). I love the emphasis on showing integrity while we teach. Slick words are never enough; they demand a humble example to back them up.

Swiss educator Johann Pestalozzi wrote, "The best way for a child to learn about God, is to know a real Christian. The best way for them to discover the power of prayer is to live with parents who pray and truly walk with God." We have been placed in our families in front of our children as examples, because we are the first Christians our children will ever see and the first to leave a primary imprint on their heart. Children have been hardwired by the

Creator to imitate mom and dad, like an ongoing game of "Follow the Leader." Christian parents must take hold of this incredible privilege of modeling the Gospel before their children.

## 2. Christian parents value and protect the sanctity of Christian marriage.

One important gift we can give our children is a good example of Christian marriage. The biblical ideal is stated in Genesis 2:24 and expanded in Ephesians 5:31, saying, "Therefore a man shall leave his father and mother and hold fast to his wife, and the two shall become one flesh." Paul continues in verse 33: "Let each one of you love his wife as himself, and let the wife see that she respects her husband." Christ, one man, one woman, love and respect— Christian parenting is built on these unchanging precepts.

Like no other time in history, Christian marriage is under attack. We like to take great pride in modern advances, but we shouldn't take pride in our so-called advancements in marriage. The damage done in countless Christian marriages should break our hearts like it does the heart of God. Let's be clear. The primary reason we must protect the marital union is because it points to the Gospel. Our marriages are to be glimpses of God's glory and a picture of Christ's love for the church, His Bride. Yes, we are recipients of the limitless blessings of marriage, but marriage isn't primarily about us. Christian marriages point to God, and therefore must be protected and valued.

The divorce rate in our culture is saddening, and the

way many married couples in the church feel that they can quit on their marriage is equally tragic. God's Word warns us repeatedly about divorce and says, "What therefore God has joined together, let not man separate" (Mark 10:9). So how seriously do Christians take this command? Meg Flammang, researcher for the Barna group, said: "We would love to be able to report that Christians are living very distinct lives and impacting the community, but . . . in the area of divorce rates they continue to be the same."[58] Marriages between two professing Christians are just as likely to end as those between two who do not claim Christ. That fact is more heartrending when research shows that children with divorced parents are much more likely to divorce themselves. The Population Reference Bureau in Washington D.C. says:

> People who experience parental divorce while growing up face an elevated risk, in adulthood, of seeing their own marriages end in divorce. . . . Our research suggests that it is the actual termination of the marriage, rather than the disturbed family relations that precede marital dissolution, that affects children's later marital stability, and that this transmission occurs mainly by undermining children's commitment to marital permanence.[59]

The casualness of divorce among Christians teaches our children that marriage isn't a lifelong covenant with God and promise to each other but instead a temporary agreement that either person can terminate. Does this mean that divorce is some sort of unforgivable sin? Of course not. Does it mean that God cannot work in divorced or blended homes? No, it doesn't. Does it mean that a wife should stay with a man who is abusive to her and the kids? That is not what I am saying. The point is that Christian parenting must place the same importance on marriage that the Bible places. We must understand a healthy marriage is the foundation of healthy parenting that enables God's glory to be seen by our children and others. Christian parents should understand the privilege they have to model God's love and grace in how they protect and value Christian marriage.

### 3. Christian parents see their children as blessings.

Your child is a blessing from God. It's true, even though many today have forgotten that children are blessings. "Behold, children are a heritage from the LORD, the fruit of the womb a reward. Blessed is the man who fills his quiver with them!" (Psalm 127:3, 5). Good parents love their kids. Godly parents understand that they are an incredible blessing from God.

It's no secret that our culture and world views children differently than fifty years ago. Newlyweds want to make sure they have protection. Protection from what? God's blessing of children? Kind of backwards, isn't it? This also is seen in the backlog of God-loving couples waiting to adopt, while thousands of lives are being aborted daily. It is seen even in how mothers who desire to stay home with their children are almost looked at with disdain and asked,

"Do you really think you will be happy doing that *all* day, *every* day?" There is an accepted view that children are an inconvenience even among married couples. Children interfere with our preferred lifestyle. Some parents openly declare that they "just can't wait" until their children are out of the house. The most recent studies have shown that children cost on average between $143,000 and $289,000.[60] Admittedly, children are a huge responsibility and, yes, very expensive. But are they a blessing or a bother? Dennis and Barbara Rainey say:

> Many parents today feel like kids are a burden. That's not what the Bible calls them. It doesn't say, "Behold, children are a burden of the Lord," or "Burdened is the man whose quiver is full of them." Our views have become distorted. What we see as a burden, God sees as a blessing. Some of us need to knock the windows out of our corrupted views and let the Spirit of God come into our homes and refresh our hearts and minds so we can see clearly again that children are a blessing.[61]

One day—sooner than we think—those muddy footprints, those marks on the wall, the spilled red Kool-Aid stains and piles of dirty diapers will be the things of the past that we miss. The late-night study sessions, the teenage drama, watching your son drive away while you quietly pray for his safety, and the soul-searching conversations will be over. As James reminds us, even these moments will be gone like a mist (James 4:14). The house will be quiet. And we will hope for a phone call from those children we don't see as often as we'd like. We cannot look past the blessing of the parenting years and the unparalleled privilege we have as parents to show our children they are our blessings.

## 4. Christian parents desire that Jesus captivate their children's hearts.

What is the goal of parenting? To raise good, respectful kids? To raise kids who have good character and strong morals? To raise the next Tiger Woods or Bill Gates? To raise doctors and lawyers and such? These are the goals of many parents whether they admit it or not. The things of this world may seem bright and attractive, but these are the fleeting things that Jesus warned us about. We must decide if our goal is to settle for good kids or aim for truly godly kids. The goal of Christian parents is to see our children captivated by Jesus. A Christian parent wants nothing more than to see his or her child live for Jesus. John Angell James says, "The chief end of every Christian parent must be the spiritual interests, the religious character, the eternal salvation of his children."[62]

Proverbs 20:7 says, "The righteous who walks in his integrity—blessed are his children after him!" Psalm 78:4–7 says:

We will not hide [these truths] from their children, but tell to the coming generation the glorious deeds of the LORD, and his might, and the wonders that he has done.

He established a testimony in Jacob and appointed a law in Israel, which he commanded our fathers to teach to their children, that the next generation might know them, the children yet unborn, and arise and tell them to their children, so that they should set their hope in God and not forget the works of God, but keep his commandments.

We want our children and grandchildren and great-grandchildren and all others after them to be captivated by Jesus. They must see His death on the cross as the most tragic and glorious event in history. They must acknowledge that Christ's death took their sin and gave them their righteous standing before God the Father with an eternal hope in Him. This is more important than what university they will attend, what career they choose, how much money they will make, or their favorite sport. We want our sons' and daughters' hearts to be dedicated to Christ alone.

One question we must wrestle with is, how much of Christ do we want to see our children possess? Enough to lead them to an obscure mission field? Enough to compel them to give all they possess to the needy and the forgotten? Enough of Christ to have a boldness that some might consider fanatical or that might lead to persecution? Christ isn't calling our children and us to an easy belief that affects a small part of our lives. He calls us to pick up our cross and follow Him (Matthew 16:24), being completely consumed by Him.

I recently spoke to a dad who was very concerned about his son's decisions since high school graduation. His son had been out of school for two years and although he had said he was going to college, he had not even applied. "His mom and I are very concerned about what this might mean for his future. Thanks for asking about him, but right now he is just working at a pet store, and it appears his life is heading nowhere. We just want the best for him but..." Not once was there any mention of his spiritual condition, not once was it mentioned if the Lord was a priority in his life, and not once was the goal that I know this parent would say was the "most important thing" (that his son loves Jesus) ever mentioned. It's almost like we have assumed the world's goals for our children is what is in their best interest. Grow up, go to college, meet someone special, marry, have kids, and that's it? Is that the ultimate vision of Christian parenting? In the efforts of providing for our children so that "they will have it better off than we did," have we asked what "better" is? Is "better" a nicer car, entrance into a more prestigious university, a higher-paying job, a more secure job, a bigger house, more comfort, less suffering? Don't get me wrong; we probably all want these things at some point for our children, but I don't think any of us would desire these things over the most important thing. What if "better off" meant a better hunger and thirst for righteousness? What about a better prayer life that shows great dependency on the Creator of our children's souls? What about a child who better understands the biblical principles that guide our lives? What about a better compassion for a world that does not know Christ as Savior and Lord? That is the kind of better I hope for. I know you and I share these values, but we cannot accept the lesser goal of good parenting, when we can strive for godly parenting. Christian parents must understand the unparalleled privilege they have to watch their children's hearts become captivated by Jesus' love.

## How Do These Distinctive Marks Change Our Parenting?

You may be thinking that I'm some sort of religious fanatic or that I'm not in the real world. You may question, "Are his kids engaged in life?" Just so you know, our kids do live in the real world. If you knew me, you'd say I was anything but a legalist. Tina and I both desire desperately that our children walk with the Lord, but just as you do, we live in the real world of study sessions until after midnight, wrecked cars, temptation and failure, and the heartache of losses, monotony of three kids needing to be four different places, and so on. I know what the real world looks like, but I would rather my daughter and sons love Jesus than be straight-A students, scholarship athletes, or class presidents. I want godly kids, not just good ones. That is what makes Christian parenting different than what the world wants for their children. That is the difference between good parenting and godly parenting.

A few years ago Dave, a dad in my ministry, came to see me because it was clear to him and everyone else that his son, Paxton, was drifting from him and also from the Lord. He said that for the first time the way his family viewed life and the way Paxton viewed life were no longer the same. Paxton was becoming attracted to the things of this world; his heart was being captivated by this world that promised so much. He was slowly abandoning his faith and his family. Dave saw the direction his son was headed and knew that something had to be done to rescue his son's relationships with God and his family.

Dave went out and bought an old Camaro that could be turned into a classic car with a lot of sweat and a lot of hours. But the car was never the point for Dave. He knew the restoration project would take countless hours. Hours spent with his son. This wise dad had the right goal in sight: restoring the relationship for the purpose of restoring his heart was more important than restoring the car. It took three years of long nights, skinned knuckles, and sore backs, but Dave said it was the best time he'd ever spent. I'll never forget the day Dave and Paxton called my boys and me over to drive to our church to do doughnuts in the parking lot. They also invited us over for a cookout and took us all for a ride in the fully restored Camaro. The car was fantastic, but the most incredible sight of the day was seeing a relationship restored between a dad and son. I thank God that He allowed me to see Luke 1:17 come to life—watching the heart of a father and the heart of a son be turned toward each other. When I talked to Dave, he had some advice for people in this same circumstance. He suggested finding help and coming up with a plan. He said, "There will be some time required. Some effort and planning will be required. Keep praying, but don't be surprised if you end up with a stronger relationship with God, your spouse, and your teenager."

Honestly, Paxton was rebelling, and his dad loved him anyway. He decided that just as he received grace from God, he would show grace to his son. Just as God went after him while he was a sinner, he sought after his son. Dave applied grace to his parenting. If we have been forgiven much, then we must also love much. Luke 7:47 says, "I tell you, her sins, which are many, are forgiven—for she loved much. But he who is forgiven little, loves little." Because you and I have received much grace, then we must be willing to apply much grace to our children. This kind of grace separates good parenting from godly parenting. That kind of grace changed each of us when we were saved, it changed Paxton, and it can change your children for eternity.

# A Parent's Tasks: Foundations of Christian Parenting

My youngest son, Tyler, plays West Raleigh Baseball. It's an excellent instructional and competitive baseball program near where we live. A couple of years ago our twelve-year old little league team was the Cal Ripken U.S. Champion and made it to the finals of the Cal Ripken World Championships. Not bad! It amazes me every year to go to the first practice of our new fall and spring teams. The coach stands up, regardless of which coach we have that year, and gives his speech. He doesn't mince words. He tells the children and parents what is expected:

1. "We are a four-night-a-week program. Two games and two practices. No exceptions. Be here."
2. "Here are your raffle tickets. You will either sell them all, or just give us the money to cover them all. It is up to you."
3. "We are going to need three more coaches for four days a week, two hours a day."

4. "We need one of you to keep the books for the games."

5. "We need one of you to be our Web administrator."

6. "We need one of you to run the public announcements every other game."

7. "Each parent will have two nights during the season to run the concession stands."

8. "We need a team mom to help with all team communications and to help line up practice fields."

9. "If you have complaints please bring it to us and not everybody else. If you are unhappy, help more or sign up to coach next time around."

Remember, this is Little League baseball. They don't weasel into asking for help. They state it up front with no apologies: "Your involvement is required."

How would you respond if your church came to you with that level of expectation? As a student pastor, I often feel guilty about asking parents for help because they all are so busy. But the truth of the matter is parents really aren't as busy as we think we are, and I have proof. Every day and every week we get our kids to those things we value. It may be 6:00 a.m. summer football practice, out-of-state soccer competitions, a seminar that puts them ahead for college, the TV show we never fail to see, the can't-miss party, the concert that we might second mortgage our house to get tickets for—you name it; we get them there if we value it, no matter the distance, no matter the cost, no matter how hard it is to pull off. The problem with many of us parents isn't our calendar or checkbook but our value system.

Christian parenting places the highest value where the Bible places the highest value on the things that are lasting.

As stated earlier, there is a distinct difference between good parenting and godly parenting, between Christian and non-Christian parenting. If what we value is different than the world and how we understand parenting is different, then the principles that guide us must also be different. I have spent quite a bit of time looking in the Word for what it teaches about parenting, and I believe it is as clear as our Little League coach. The Bible plainly lays out principles that must guide everything we do. These principles apply to every parent in every situation, and can impact any parent-child relationship. If your child is a prodigal or at church every time the doors are open; if your daughter is seven or seventeen; if your son never kept a secret from you or only speaks to you in grunts, remember there are biblical principles that lay a solid foundation. They are not a simplistic plan or empty promises that don't work in real life. The Bible gives us concrete principles that work. They may sound familiar to you, but there is a difference between knowing something and doing it. The question we all have to answer is: Are we doing the things that are laid out in the Scriptures?

Here are eight essential principles from the pages of Scripture.

## 1. Pray with and for our children.

I know. You've heard this a thousand times. It may even sound simplistic or cliché. But are we doing it? Some things are important enough to be said over and over, and praying with and for our kids is one of them. Philippians 4:6 reminds us, "In everything by prayer and supplication with thanksgiving let your requests be made known to God." It is the task of a parent to model this attitude toward prayer to their children.

Do we really believe in prayer? Do we believe that our children's lives will be different because of our prayers? Do we believe that God will protect them? When was the last time we got on our knees—or better yet, on our faces—with our children and really poured out our hearts to the Almighty? I am talking about prayers that are more than thirty-second blessings before downing a chicken potpie. I am talking about inviting our children to pray with us in faith matters, praying prayers that only God can answer. Inviting them to take part in deep, soul groaning before the sovereign God. Inviting them into the throne room of God.

I have the privilege of hosting a Bible study for eighth-grade boys at my home on Wednesday nights. Midway through the year we made a list of prayers that only God could answer. Things bigger than us. God-sized tasks. These young men have watched God graciously begin to answer these prayers, and they can't wait to get on their knees each week. I have seen it firsthand. Children like yours and mine are ready for these kinds of prayers and hungry to pray them.

This kind of praying teaches our sons and daughters vital lessons. It teaches them that God answers prayer and models for them dependence. It helps them apply faith and teaches them where to go with concerns. We cannot allow our kids to think that all they have to do is run to mom and dad to fix all their problems. Mom and dad can't always do that. We have to model for them what it means to go to the true source of wisdom, strength, and help: the Almighty God.

## 2. Continually give our children back to God.

In 1 Samuel 1:27–28, Hannah says, "For this child I prayed, and the LORD has granted me my petition that I made to him. Therefore I have lent him to the LORD. As long as he lives, he is lent to the LORD." What a powerful prayer, one that every parent should pray daily.

Our job is to point our children to Christ, but we cannot make them believe. That is ultimately between God and our children. J. C. Ryle wisely reminds us:

> I know that you cannot convert your child. I know well that they who are born again are born, not of the will of man, but of God. But I also know that God says expressly, "Train up a child in the way he should go," and that He never laid a command on man which He would not give man grace to perform. . . . We have only to do as the servants commanded at the marriage feast in Cana, to fill the water-pots with water, and we may safely leave it to the Lord to turn that water into wine.[63]

Maybe you remember standing at a baby dedication, reciting a promise with your pastor to give your child to the Lord. Maybe, like many other aspects of the Christian walk, you have since realized that surrendering this gift is a continual process, not a one-and-done proposition that you can check off your list of parental duties. Do you remember the first day of school for your child? Remember the first day they drove off in their car? Remember their first date or when they left for college? Have you stood at the altar ready to give your daughter away? Believe me, giving our children away isn't something we do just at these milestones. Giving these great gifts back to the Lord is a daily process.

Maybe your child is wayward. Give him to the Lord. Maybe she is forming some new relationships that you worry about. Give her to the Lord. Maybe he is wrestling with his future plans. Give him to the Lord. Maybe she seems to be on track. Give her to the Lord. Every day we should pray to God, acknowledge that He gave our children to us, and place them back into the loving Father's hands. Only He can change their hearts and give them purpose, so we must give them back to Him each day.

### 3. Embrace our God-given role as daily mentors.

Have you ever tried to keep a journal for one of your children? This is a common practice in our ministry and it takes a lot of discipline and soul searching. Solomon wrote three books of the Bible. Ever read his love letters to his bride (Song of Solomon)? Whoa! Ever read his journal to his son? In Proverbs, he clearly states the recipient of this work, mentioning him thirty-nine times as "son." Twenty-three of these references to sons actually read "my son" (Proverbs 1:8; 2:1; 3:1, for examples). Solomon knew his spiritual legacy would be passed down specifically through his children and he wasn't about to abdicate this role to anyone. His message and his children were more important than any encumbrances that he would have to push through. He knew there were real dangers and he wanted his children to have a roadmap for life. He wanted them to know what pleased the Lord and which pitfalls to avoid. For many of us today the opposite is true. Sure, we see the need, but we conveniently and mistakenly assume that someone else is going to do this job for us.

We live in a society that has become increasingly specialized in providing services. You name it and you can pay someone to do it for you. Just open up the phone book to find someone to wash your dog, clean your gutters, buy your groceries, tutor your children, or watch your kids. Unfortunately, some parents and churches view children and student ministries in the same way—as a spiritual drop-off service best left to the professionals. These parents think their only responsibility is to take their child to church and put him or her in a spiritual environment and the result will be a morally sound, young adult. Then they are angry when things do not turn out as expected and demand an explanation from a pastor they barely know or may have never met. What's missing from this scenario?

Nowhere in the Bible does it say that it is the church's job to be the lone discipler of young people. Instead, the Bible places the emphasis on the parents. Of course, the church should support and echo what the parents are doing, but it cannot and should not assume the exclusive responsibility to disciple children. The parents' role is to be daily mentors to their children, always pointing their children to the Savior with the words they say and the life they lead. That is a privilege that I would never want to give to a children's or youth pastor. That is my role, and I am thankful for it. I want to say with the same confidence of Joshua: "As for me and my house, we will serve the LORD" (Joshua 24:15).

### 4. Look for invitations to join God's work.

We must use any and every opportunity to point our children to Christ. God is always working in our children's lives and often He invites us to join Him. We can use these moments to help our children gain an eternal perspective, more than the here-and-now drudgery of life.

Some moments are obvious, already on your calendar, waiting for you to take advantage of them (Christmas, Easter, birthdays, graduation). God encourages us to plan for these specific events. In Jewish tradition, they have numerous festivals, such as the highly symbolic Passover meal. These symbols and traditions were meant to spark conversation. Deuteronomy 6:20 says, "When your son asks you in time to come, 'What is the meaning of the testimonies and the statutes and the rules that the LORD our God has commanded you?'" Children in ancient Israel were no different than children today in that they ask about what is going on around them. I remember my children being inquisitive toddlers with thousands of questions. All the *why* questions are still ringing in my ears. You can either let their questions drive you crazy, or you can use them for the Lord. Our children's questions and curiosity are opportunities. They are invitations to join God's work. Notice how the passage continues: "Then you shall say to your son, 'We were Pharaoh's slaves in Egypt. And the LORD brought us out of Egypt with a mighty hand. . . . And it will be righteousness for us, if we are careful to do all this commandment before the LORD our God, as he has commanded us'" (verses 21, 25). This passage tells us to use our children's questions to explain key truths and share our faith stories. They are divine appointments He sends our way.

However, we can't plan for all of the questions asked by our children, because they often show up when we least expect them. These are opportunities God creates for us in everyday life so we can use them to talk about Him, His creation, His ways, and His plan for our lives. For the moments that we can't plan, we must instead prepare. There is a difference between planning and preparing. Planned events can be calendared, but for all the unexpected curveballs, we must daily prepare ourselves.

Here's a personal example of a moment I could never have planned. Several years ago my son and I stood in line at Taco Bell. We had only a few minutes between practice and an appointment and we were in a hurry. As I was getting our food and trying to maneuver around the people, William, my son, leaned in and asked me this question: "Dad, what is the difference between sex and oral sex?" Did I mention about the people standing around? Did I mention the topic? I'm glad he came to me rather than asking some kid at the school lunch table, but I almost dropped my chalupas. It seems that questions like that often do catch us off guard. Many times those teaching moments come when we least expect it, but precisely when God ordained them to occur. We can't plan on these moments, but we can prepare for them.

What unplanned invitations from God will you encounter today? Ink on the sofa, a messy room, an ignored chore, a forgotten curfew, a missing credit card your child borrowed—these are opportunities. These are random moments that appear late at night after a hard day. When our sons forget to tell us about a school project, we can either get frustrated or use it as a teaching tool. When our daughters get angry about their clothes right before you walk out the door to church, we can either match the volume level, or calm down and take the time to explain how God cares more about a heart than a sundress. Our response to these moments depends on your personal preparation. In these times you and I need a quick recall of just how much grace God has extended toward us, and then extend that same grace toward our children.

Is God's Word so indwelling our lives that we can use these opportunities to point them to the Gospel of Christ? When I'm angry there is no time to stop, read a few chapters of the Bible, and find a verse to change my perspective. Those moments call for parents who have been prepared by reading His Word daily, saturating their minds and being ready to be used when He invites them to join in His work.

## 5. Practice unfailing love.

Each year our church hosts an event called Joy Prom for people with special needs. These incredible, special-needs people enjoy a prom just for themselves where they dress up, get a makeover, dance, have their pictures taken, and are given the royal treatment throughout the night. Each year I serve as a greeter and am continually humbled and blessed as I see many moms and dads lift their children out of the car and into wheelchairs. I watch parents handle embarrassing and unpleasant medical problems with grace and ease. These parents are examples for me of how I want to parent. I want to have that kind of selfless love for my children.

A parent's love should be an unfailing, Gospel-centered kind of love. We are all moved to tears when we see parents care for their physically sick or special-needs children, but what if the sickness isn't physical? What if it is a spiritual problem of rebellion? What if it is a relational problem of choosing unhealthy friendships? Do we show the same type of unfailing love?

I speak weekly with parents who are going through tough seasons with their children, and how they respond varies greatly. I have seen parents wash their hands of any responsibility and heard some say, "I can't wait until my child is old enough to leave home" as if there were some magical disappearance of the parent/child responsibility. You can read the Bible from cover to cover and you will never find such an escape clause, because it doesn't exist.

I have also seen parents battle for the souls of their children. I have seen parents resolve to protect, defend, and provide unfailing love even when it was met with a stiff lip and a bowed back. I have seen parents who daily pray for the prodigal to come back home. I have seen them keep every line of communication open, even when the children are clearly in sinful lifestyles. Why? Because they refuse to give up on their children and refuse to lose the last bit of influence they have to point them to the Savior. They won't stop fighting for, praying for, and loving their children because they realize the spiritual battle their children are fighting.

Proverbs 17:17 says, "A friend loves at all times, and a brother is born for adversity." How much more should a parent love at all times? We cannot ever give up on our children, even when their actions break our hearts and the heart of God. Ephesians 5 begins, "Therefore be imitators of God, as beloved children. And walk in love, as Christ loved us and gave himself up for us, a fragrant offering and sacrifice to God" (vv. 1–2). While I was a sinner, rebelling against my heavenly Father, He didn't give up on me. He sent His Son to die for me. He put people in my path whom He used to turn my life toward Him. The Father's unfailing love is our example. We must learn to love our children with this kind of love.

## 6. Embrace a relational view of parenting.

Would you say you are friends with your children? I understand that I am first a father to my children before I am a friend to them, but I also hope to have an open, welcoming relationship with my kids. While there is a danger in striving to be friends and lose all authority, I aim to have relationship and authority. Jesus modeled this kind of relationship. He possessed all the authority of God incarnate but said to His disciples in John 15:15, "No longer do I call you servants, for the servant does not know what his master is doing; but I have called you friends, for all that I have heard from my Father I have made known to you." Psalm 103:13 gives us a picture of relational parenting: "As a father shows compassion to his children, so the LORD shows compassion to those who fear him." Paul echoes this same picture of relational parenting: "But we were gentle among you, like a nursing mother taking care of her own children. ...For you know how, like a father with his children, we exhorted each one of you and encouraged you and charged you to walk in a manner worthy of God" (1 Thessalonians 2:7, 11–12).

When our children are younger, we are obviously in more of an authoritative role. When was the last time you had a meaningful conversation with your two-year-old? We pick them up when they cry, tell them no when they are disobeying, and don't need to do much explaining. As our children mature, the relational aspect of parenting becomes crucial. Dr. Wes Black says, "Parents need help in adjusting their parenting style as their adolescent grows toward young adulthood. Parents need help in the transition of their role from 'parent' to 'adult friend' for their maturing adolescent." [64]

A relational view of parenting keeps the future in clear view. If you came home from work one day and loaded your family in a car and started barking out one hundred rules for a road trip, you would quickly face mutiny. We are all are wired to want to know where we are going. We need to buy into a vision that allows us to make sense of it all. This is also true in parenting. Many times we get on to our children about their messy rooms, grades, friends, lack of gratitude, lack of discipline . . . and the list goes on. They blow up, we blow up, the conversation is over, and the relationship is severed. We seldom take the time to explain the reason their behavior doesn't lead to God's redemptive plan for their lives. We assume their young minds understand this, but they often don't. It takes time to explain where these attitudes or behaviors will take them in the future. Healthy relationships take time, and we have to build strong relationships to make sure the door stays open, so when our children need godly wisdom, they will come to us.

There's a lot of research pointing to the importance of a healthy relationship between parent and child:

- "Parents are the single most important influence on children's decision to smoke, drink, or use drugs, yet many parents do not fully understand the extent of their influence."[65]

- "Adolescents who reported a 'connectedness' to their parents were the least likely to engage in risky behaviors. These adolescents felt close to their parents, believed their parents and family members cared for them, and were satisfied with their family relationships."[66]

- "Among teens who have dinner with their families five or more nights in a typical week, 86 percent report that they have never tried cigarettes, compared with 65 percent of those teens who have dinner with their families two nights a week or less."[67]

- "Hands-on parents—parents who establish a household culture where they consistently set down rules and expectations for their teen's behavior and monitor what their teen does—have teens at substantially lower risk of smoking, drinking and using illegal drugs than the average teen."[68]

- People seem to intuitively "know" that parents have an impact on children. For the most part, research supports what people already know: parents are, indeed, the largest influence on how children think, feel, and act.[69]

- Research and common sense tell us that emotional and cognitive development is fostered through relationships with parents.[70]

This relationship between parents and child is so critical because it points to a greater relationship our children will have with the heavenly Father. He has called His children friends. We can do the same.

### 7. Envision parenting as generational.

When was the last time you studied genealogy in the Bible? (Try to control your excitement). There are dozens of names and "begats" in Scripture, but have you ever stopped and considered why? They are there for a reason. It can be difficult to read a genealogy because it covers pages of names we don't know and can't pronounce, and frankly it's not about our families. However, Jesus would view the list in Luke 3 differently than we do today. He knew the story of Tamar's struggles. He could tell you about Rahab's courage. He was very familiar with David's failures. He understood the godly legacy left to Him by these heroes of the faith. Each name was an epic story of God being faithful to his family. The problem is that we don't see these lists like someone in a Jewish family might see them. They understand that their family and faith affect more than mom, dad, brother, and sister. More than the here and now, faith affects generations.

We don't often think about generational parenting. We don't think about a lasting legacy for Christ. We sometimes don't protect our testimony and think about how it will affect our great-great-grandchildren. We often forget that it is "God making his appeal through us" (2 Corinthians 5:20). We think that we have eighteen to twenty years in this parenting thing and we're done. Maybe you've seen the Mercedes commercial that illustrates our current cultural view. It says, "3,212 conference calls, 745 airplane trips, 1,000 of hours of lost sleep, two out of three kids raised successfully . . . it's payback time: The new E-class Mercedes."

Where some might think that two out of three isn't a bad result for child rearing, those in a Jewish family think that two out of three means that hundreds of descendants will be left without a spiritual heritage. This Hebrew concept of generational parenting can be seen as early as Abraham.

- In Genesis 18:19 Abraham understood his clear God-given assignment: "For I have chosen him, that he may command his children and his household after him to keep the way of the LORD by doing righteousness and justice."

- The second of the Ten Commandments tells us that God shows "love to thousands of those who love me and keep my commandments" (Exodus 20:6).

- Psalm 119:90 says, "Your faithfulness endures to all generations; you have established the earth, and it stands fast."

- Psalm 89:4 says, "I will establish your offspring forever, and build your throne for all generations."

- Joshua 22:27 says that the altar was to be, "a witness between us and you, and between our generations after us, that we do perform the service of the LORD in his presence with our burnt offerings and sacrifices and peace offerings, so your children will not say to our children in time to come, 'You have no portion in the LORD.'"

- Isaiah 60:15 says, "Although you have been forsaken and hated, with no one traveling through, I will make you the everlasting pride and the joy of all generations" (NIV).

Your parenting affects more than your child's here and now. It affects generations to come and their eternity.

## 8. Trust that God is growing parents, not just children.

God uses my children as the sharpest tools in His toolbox. Many of the behaviors I detest in my children I confess that I also possess: selfishness, ego, pride, irresponsibility, lack of gratitude, a temper, and more. I have heard it said that God gives you the children you need to change you. God is repeatedly using my children to shape my character. We must not fail to remember that the power of the Gospel changes us just as much as it does our children. All this Jesus stuff isn't just for eight-year-olds. I see the fact that God is growing me as a source of encouragement. God isn't through with me yet! He continues to work with me, guide me, and shape me.

Gary Thomas wrote an excellent book called Sacred Parenting where he calls our children "holy teachers" and says,

The process of parenting is one of the most spiritually formative journeys a man and woman can undertake.... The journey of caring for, raising, training, and loving children will mark us indelibly and powerfully. We cannot be the same people we once were. We will be forever changed, eternally altered. Spiritually speaking, we need to raise children every bit as much as they need us to raise them.[71]

I believe that God gives us the specific children we have to work on our hearts, just as much as theirs. Through parenting we are growing and changing right alongside our toddlers and teens. That is part of God's plan.

I hope you can learn the same thing I am learning: God isn't finished with me yet. I am nowhere near the perfect parent, so I have hope when I know that my Father is teaching me how to be a father. I have the perfect example to learn from, and He is active, continually shaping me into the dad He created me to be. He is doing the same for you. In James 1:5, He promises to give us wisdom when we ask Him, saying, "If any of you lacks wisdom, let him ask God, who gives generously to all without reproach, and it will be given him." Trust that He will continue to give you wisdom, guidance, and encouragement in the privilege of raising your children.

## FINDING DIRECTION

I bought my wife and my sixteen-year-old daughter each a global positioning system (GPS) for Christmas. The following day, William and I left for Snowshoe, West Virginia, for our father/son passage trip (you'll hear more about passage trips in Chapter 7). I borrowed Tina's GPS, just to test its reliability, of course. I turned it on, pressed "Recreation" then "Ski Resorts" and there it was: "Snowshoe." I touched the screen, and it gave me precise directions the entire trip. I knew my destination, and the GPS got me there.

Every road takes you somewhere. If I would have turned off the GPS and left my home heading south, I would have never made it to Snowshoe. It doesn't matter how much I wanted to get to Snowshoe; heading the wrong direction won't get me there. The same is true in Christian parenting. We all should know our desired final address. We all want to get to the same place—we want our kids to be captivated by Jesus. But there are so many wrong roads we can get on, and these roads won't end up with the kids we hope to raise. There is only one GPS we can trust, and that is the Bible. It gives us clear principles that anyone can use to get where we want to go. We must allow the Word of God to determine our path.

This may be the first time you have been exposed to these principles, and you might struggle to remember them. Don't be discouraged, no matter how old your children are. You can still pray one verse daily (turning Philippians 1:9 [NIV] into a short prayer): "God, please give me wisdom and a depth of insight." You may want to put the list of principles where you can think and pray over them. Maybe you need to talk to someone at church about a principle that you struggle to apply. Do whatever it takes to get back on the right road. While it may not be easy, it is well worth it. Every path has a destination. I hope we choose the road less traveled.

======================================= 6 =======

# A PARENT'S PARTNER: HOW YOUR CHURCH CAN HELP

Bikes are one of the first really cool gifts that we receive and one of the first big steps toward independence, especially for boys. When I was six I got my first bike, and even though I could barely pedal at first, I dreamed of the places I'd go. I imagined all of the things I'd do with my junk-yard-quality bike that was made from pieces of eight different bikes handed down from cousins. I grew up in the Evil Knievel era, and I can't tell you how many wrecks I had from makeshift ramps of plywood and rocks. There is something in little boys' DNA that causes us all to try wheelies, to ride with no hands, and to invent tricks that will wow our buddies. One of the first simple tricks I mastered is one you might have tried as well. I wondered if I could pedal my bike with just one leg, and then I was amazed when I could. I could push the pedal down hard enough so that the momentum would carry it back to the top and you could push it down again. I remember riding up our dirt road, one leg burning from being overworked while the other leg did nothing. Of course you couldn't hit top speeds, and making daredevil jumps was out of the question, but it can be done. I don't know any bike owner and "wannabe-Knievel" who hasn't tried this small but important bike feat.

The bike pedal and cranks as you know them were invented in 1861. They are simple in their mechanics, but modern technology has yet to improve on the basic design of two pedals working together to maximize the effectiveness. I tell you this because the two bike pedals serve as a simple illustration of a much bigger concept and a much greater design—God's design for discipleship. According to Scripture, God formed two institutions that work together like the two pedals—the family and the church—both have the task of discipleship. The first institution is seen in Genesis and throughout the Old Testament when God created the first families and gave the parents the task of discipling children (Deuteronomy 6:4–8). The second institution, the church, is seen clearly in the New Testament with God giving her the purpose of making disciples (Matthew 28:19–20). These two institutions, like two pedals of a bike, are interdependent on the other to accomplish the task of discipleship. Sadly, in many contexts today, the family and the church operate without being connected to each other. This leaves the church or a pastor pushing the spiritual pedal of discipleship making the overall process nowhere near effective. Below is another great picture of the two institutions:

> The Christian church and the Christian home as institutions are closely bound together. They are like Siamese

twins: if you cut them apart you may sever an artery of life and cause one or both to die. The church cannot function as she should in a disordered world unless she employs the home as her main reliance in Christian nurture. And I feel certain that the family cannot be a Christian family or a happy family unless it stays in the circulation of those spiritual influences of which the church is the great custodian.[72]

The family and the church were created to work together, but in many cases they do not. As a result we find Christian families today disintegrating and more young people fleeing the church than ever before. For us to have a biblical framework for discipling our children, we must shift our understanding to match the emphasis the Bible places on the family and the church. For too long what has been missing is a mentality that places equal importance on family *and* church. In many church contexts parents have handed over their biblically assigned task as primary disciplers to let the "professionals" teach their children about God. In other contexts, parents pull their children out of all children and youth activities and try to disciple their kids alone. Neither is biblical. Neither is ideal. The family and the church need each other, like two pedals on a bike.

## CHILDREN NEED A FAMILY

We have already looked at the Shema in Deuteronomy 6:4–9, but if the Orthodox Jews recited it twice daily, it is worth being repeated. Of all the great Old Testament passages concerning creation, faith, God's provisions, the coming Messiah, the Ten Commandments, repentance, and forgiveness, it is eye-opening that it was this passage God impressed on them to repeat, not once, but twice daily. Also, in case we missed the importance of this command the first time, the Lord repeated these same instructions to parents in Deuteronomy 11. All of this repetition is more than coincidence. It is clear that the Shema is one of the most important passages in the Old Testament, as it instructs parents with their God-given assignment to disciple:

Hear, O Israel: The LORD our God, the LORD is one. You shall love the LORD your God with all your heart and with all your soul and with all your might. And these words that I command you today shall be on your heart. You shall teach them diligently to your children, and shall talk of them when you sit in your house, and when you walk by the way, and when you lie down, and when you rise. You shall bind them as a sign on your hand, and they shall be as frontlets between your eyes. You shall write them on the doorposts of your house and on your gates. (Deuteronomy 6:4–9)

One researcher sums up this command well by saying:

The responsibility for raising spiritual champions, according to the Bible, belongs to the parents. The spiritual nurture of children is supposed to take place in the home.

Organizations and people from outside the home might support those efforts, but the responsibility is squarely laid at the feet of the family. This is not a job for specialists. It is a job for parents.[73]

Pay careful attention to the words of Dr. Tom Ascol, director of Founders Ministries:

The primary responsibility for teaching your children about God is yours, dear parent. It is not the Sunday school's, the church's, nor the pastor's. God has entrusted this important work to you. If you do not invest your time and effort to teach your children about God, be assured someone else will. The television and the theater will teach them that God, if He exists at all, is an irrelevant, indulgent being that is little more than a nice kindly old man. If you do not teach your children truth and righteousness, be assured that there are a multitude of teachers in this world who would deceive them into thinking that "truth" and morality are relative ideas and can be shaped to fit anyone's beliefs or standards.[74]

Unfortunately, many parents don't understand the role the Bible lays at their feet. They have been taught that their only real job is to drop the kids off at church and let the professionals do the teaching, but that concept is foreign to the Bible. In his book *Soul Searching*, Christian Smith concluded the largest, most in-depth research ever conducted on the spirituality of American teens and stated:

The best way to get most youth more involved in and serious about their faith communities is to get their parents more involved in and serious about their faith communities. For decades in many religious traditions, the prevailing model of youth ministry has relied on pulling teens away from their parents. In some cases, youth ministers have come to see parents as adversaries. There is no doubt a time and place for unique teen settings and activities; still, our findings suggest that overall youth ministry would probably best be pursued in larger context of family ministry, that parents should be viewed as indispensable partners in the religious formation of youth.[75]

As a parent of teens and a student pastor who works with teens, I am concerned about our misunderstanding of the need the family has for the church and the church for the family. I often wonder if perhaps we have moved so far away from the biblical ideal that we may no longer recognize it. Mark DeVries, vice president of Youth Builders, reminds us,

Effective youth ministry in the 21st century is about bringing parents back into the picture. No longer can the church act as the main dispenser of spiritual formation. We need to see ourselves as resources for parents in their roles as spiritual formation builders. It's not the job of the church to be the only force behind students' spiritual formation. It is, and always has been, the role of parents.[76]

Obviously the same can be said about effective preschool and children's ministries. Children need parents.

## CHILDREN NEED A CHURCH

There is a new term out there that keeps me awake at night: "graduating from God." This is a phrase that refers to the mass exodus of teens from the church around the time of high school graduation. Think I am exaggerating?

- A study from UCLA found that almost half of college students drift away from their Christian upbringing. While 52 percent of incoming students said that they regularly took part in church events, the number shrinks to 29 percent who are still involved in church activities by their junior year.[77]

- Josh McDowell estimates, "Over 69 percent of youth are leaving traditional church after high school."[78]

- Mark Matlock, student ministry guru, finds, "Depending on whose numbers you use, 58–84 percent of graduating youth from church youth groups are not returning [to church]."[79]

- George Barna gives troubling news in his book Real Teens: "Now only 33 percent of churched youth say that the church will play a part in their lives when they leave home."[80]

- Glenn Schultz at LifeWay Christian Resources estimates that 75 percent of young people leave church in their late teens and aren't reconnecting later.[81]

- Student Venture reports that about 70 percent of seniors in high school who claimed faith stop attending church during the college years.[82]

We have plenty of young people staying very busy in our churches. We have Vacation Bible Schools, Sunday schools, retreats, lock-ins, after-school programs, children's worship, preteen-only worship, teen-only worship, day trips, overnight trips, weeklong trips, camps, and entire buildings or wings dedicated to age groups. It makes you wonder if our young people are learning to love these programs or learning to love Christ and His Bride, the church. Today's consumer-mentality approach leaves young people asking, "How does the church serve me?" rather than "How can I serve the church?"

Young people somehow are beginning to believe that they can love God and love Jesus, but not the church. That's not possible. That is the same as saying, "Steve, I love you, but I can't stand your wife." The church is Christ's Bride. If our children love Christ, the natural progression would be that they also fall in love with the Bride of Christ, the church. Josh Harris says, "The greatest motivation we could ever find for being passionately committed to the Church is that Jesus is passionately committed to the Church. . . . If Jesus loves the Church, you and I should too. It's that simple."[83]

The first time Christ ever spoke of the church, His Bride, is found in Matthew 16:15–18 as He talked with disciples and asked:

> He said to them, "But who do you say that I am?" Simon Peter replied, "You are the Christ, the Son of the living God." And Jesus answered him, "Blessed are you, Simon Bar-Jonah! For flesh and blood has not revealed this to you, but my Father who is in heaven. And I tell you, you are Peter, and on this rock I will build my church, and the gates of hell shall not prevail against it."

Not only is this the first time Jesus spoke of His Bride, but He also offered a promise that nothing, not even hell itself, will be able to overcome her. The church is that important to God.

While Jesus' words promised that the church was coming, its beginning was carefully chronicled for us in Acts 2. It is important to note that the beginning of the church was marked with miracles, speaking in foreign languages and thousands saved daily. This is important because it shows that God started the church, not the disciples. The church was ordained by God and given an important role on earth and for eternity. Also, notice what the start of the church was like at the end of Acts 2:

> They devoted themselves to the apostles' teaching and to the fellowship, to the breaking of bread and to prayer. Everyone was filled with awe, and many wonders and mi-

raculous signs were done by the apostles. All the believers were together and had everything in common. Selling their possessions and goods, they gave to anyone as he had need. Every day they continued to meet together in the temple courts. They broke bread in their homes and ate together with glad and sincere hearts, praising God and enjoying the favor of all the people. And the Lord added to their number daily those who were being saved. (verses 42–47)

Notice the relationship between home and church; there was no division between the two. What happened in church moved into the home, and vice versa. And what result did we see from the continuation of truth being taught from the church and into the home? The Lord blessed and people were saved. Regrettably, the two have drifted apart and our current model of ministry has come to accept, if not promote, the division. Maybe we have lost what the church understood two thousand years ago—its vital role of supporting and championing the family. As George Barna notes, "The greatest influence a church may have in affecting children is by impacting their parents."[84] He also says:

Unlike parents who embrace the "dump and run" strategy of spiritual nurturing—dump the kids at church, run off until the allotted time has expired, then wait until next week to repeat the process to provide their offspring with their dose of spiritual experience—revolutionary parents see their church as an invaluable partner in a long-term effort to raise a mature follower of Christ.[85]

A parental drop-off approach might at best keep kids busy in church for a few years, but it usually doesn't lead to lasting faith in their adult years.

The church is an important part of God's plan, and so is the family. Christ loved His Bride and ordained her with several purposes that are laid out differently in Scripture than the purposes for the family are laid out. It is easy to understand the church's responsibility to disciple adults, but notice that both institutions have been given the task to disciple young people. Why the overlap? Those of you around kids often can see God's wisdom in that plan. As I have said, it is clear that the primary task of discipling children falls on parents, and I believe that the church must take its equipping role. I am not saying we need to abolish church ministry to children or teens—quite the opposite. I believe the church has an important role in their lives. I could write an entire chapter about these roles. Below are a few reasons why the church and its ministries to young people are needed:

- The church is needed to surround young people with godly adults who can provide love and care, truth they can build their lives on, and a model to follow (1 Corinthians 11:1; 1 Peter 5:2).

- The church is needed to reach out to and model Christianity to children who do not have Christian parents (Matthew 19:14; 28:19–20).

- The church is needed to reinforce a biblical worldview. We have all seen how a young person will sometimes listen to a volunteer or Bible study leader, even though they have heard the same truth from their parent (2 Timothy 4:2).

- The church is needed to be a neutral third party serving as an impartial advisor between parents and children, bringing about reconciliation when needed (2 Corinthians 5:18).

- The church is needed to connect young people with other Christians who support, encourage, and keep them accountable (Hebrews 10:25).

- The church is needed to provide opportunities for young people to use and sharpen their gifts while serving the body of Christ (1 Corinthians 12).

- The church is needed because it is the pillar of truth and sound doctrine for the entire world (1 Timothy 3:15).

- The church is needed because spiritual growth in the New Testament generally happens within the context of the church (Ephesians 4:11–16).

It is clear that partnership between church and home is God's plan, God's wisdom, God's design. He put these two institutions in place for our good and His glory, and any framework or plan that ignores these two institutions is foolishness. While it may sound familiar, it seems to me that we have ignored these principles for so long that we have forgotten the power in them. Church and family must work together. There is no other biblical option.

## Parents Need the Church

I can't speak for you, but I need the church. I can't even imagine what my family would look like if it weren't for others in church teaching, encouraging, and training me. Robert Clark, Joanne Brubaker, and Roy Zuck say it this way:

> [Children and teen ministries] should be church related and family centered. The task of the church is to make the whole ethos of the home evangelical in spirit and practice. ...The home is responsible for training children, but the church is responsible for equipping parents in how to train their children.[86]

The responsibility to teach our children the incredible truths of God may seem overwhelming, but the Bride of Christ is there to help. She will teach you how to teach. She will train you how to train. You cannot do it alone.

Do you remember the uncertainty of your first bike ride? I remember depending on the training wheels, knowing that if they were removed I would wobble and crash. I clearly remember the day my dad took the training wheels off of my bike. I was at my grandma's house. I was scared,

Mom was scared, and Grandma was scared. Everyone but Dad. He wasn't scared because he was holding on to my bike and running alongside me to help me succeed. He must have run around my grandma's house twenty-five times with me that night. He supported me. He guided me. He protected me. If I had crashed, he would have helped. It would have been impossible for me to have done it without him.

God showed us great grace when He blessed us with the church, His Bride. She is our partner in the task of discipleship. We cannot do it without her. Like my dad teaching me to ride my bike, the church reaches out, supports, guides, protects. If we crash, the church will be there to help the healing begin. God gave us the church because we need the church. We cannot do it without her.

Later on that night after Dad's lesson on riding a bike, I lay in bed encouraged by the success he helped me achieve. The next morning I got up early and pulled the bike out of the garage. That morning, I reached my goal. I rode it by myself—a task I could have never achieved by myself. Some things I cannot do alone. I cannot change a heart. I cannot forgive sin. I cannot get someone into heaven. But Christ can. Praise be to God, because He gave us the church, which proclaims God "who is able to do far more abundantly than all that we ask or think, according to the power at work within us, to him be glory in the church and in Christ Jesus throughout all generations, forever and ever. Amen" (Ephesians 3:20–21).

# A Parent's Tools: Real Ideas to Make Discipleship Happen

Did you ever play hooky from school when you were growing up? I did. Of course I felt really bad when I was telling my mom I was sick and was sure I couldn't make it through a demanding day at school. However, as soon as my brother and sister left the house, a sudden, almost miracle occurred—all that had been ailing me would disappear—my temperature would drop, my stomach would stop aching, and my energy would return.

In the fall of my sixth-grade year I awoke and immediately knew I wouldn't be able to make it to school. One reason I remember this day so well was it just so happened to be my birthday. It seemed my dad had the same bug that day, because he decided he couldn't go to work either. After breakfast Dad asked me to get dressed because he needed me to help him with an errand. Thirty minutes later we found ourselves standing in the middle of man-heaven. We were in a gun shop surrounded by what seemed to be a million guns, especially to a twelve-year-old boy. Noticing the drool on our chins, a salesperson approached and asked if he could be of service. My dad's words that day will be forever etched on my heart. He said, "Today is my son's birthday; he will be a man soon and he is going to need his own gun." These are the kind of words that every son longs to hear from his dad. Today, I still have the Ithaca 20-gauge, pump shotgun he bought me, but more importantly I possess a legacy of manhood that has been passed down from my dad that I hope to pass to my sons.

Unfortunately I have seen the other side of this story many times throughout my adult life. My profession as a pastor to young people and families has provided a unique front-row seat for more than twenty years. I have watched lives wrecked when children have no parent battling for them daily. Research reveals the following:

- Twenty-eight million children live in fatherless homes in America.[87]
- Seventy-seven percent of children are classified as latchkey kids.[88]
- Six and a half million children are raised by grandparents or other relatives.[89]

In case you missed the news alert, families are under attack.

Perhaps even more troublesome than the absent mother and father, might be the present-but-distracted mother or father. These are the parents who come home but aren't engaged; they are physically present but not emotionally or relationally. They are there for their kids, but not entirely there. They listen, but not fully. They know when their kids are hurting, sometimes. It is tragic.

On the other hand, there are also overbearing parents who seem to care about their children, but ultimately care only about themselves. They are involved but drive a greater wedge between them and the rest of their family. Let me illustrate how deceptive this involved-parent illusion can be, because it looks like very active parenting. Last season my youngest son had a Little League game. In the first inning, a player on the other team made an error and his coach, who was also his dad, became irate. After the inning the dad berated his son for several minutes in front of the other boys on his team and told him to sit on the bench for the rest of the game. Around the third inning the dad shouted at his son and told him, "Go to the concession stand because that is where people like you end up anyways—making hot dogs for the real athletes." These words were piercing arrows that wounded this boy. You could see it in his body language as he sat at the end of the bench, put his head in his hands, and cried for the last few innings. I really don't think this dad started coaching his son so that he could crush him in a way that he might never recover. While others in the league may applaud this dad's involvement, his son sees through the illusion with tear-filled eyes, not able to lift his head to applaud. I would like to think that this dad eventually apologized to his son. I pray that God would give this dad grace to humble himself before his son and ask forgiveness.

Could you imagine the price of a front-row seat to the World Series or Super Bowl? As a dad and pastor, God has given me a very unique seat as both dad and pastor to young people and their families. My front-row seat into people's lives is priceless. It has been humbling, educational, depressing, amusing, shocking, beautiful, agonizing, heartbreaking, exhilarating, encouraging, and even numbing at times. That is why I can assure you that, while it may not have always been pleasant, I have sat with my eyes *wide open.* For over twenty years I have taken notes from those parents who are engaged and seek to impart truth into their children's lives for today and for eternity.

Like skilled craftsmen who work with great focus to shape a priceless piece of art, these parents shape, teach, and endure with great patience, almost never taking for granted their apparent privilege. I have seen their children rise up and call them blessed. I have seen these parents faithfully walk for over three decades with their prodigal children. I have seen incredible habits on display that I have adopted and have encouraged others to adopt. I have learned much from them, and the goal of this chapter is to share some lessons I have learned.

## Why Bring Discipleship Home?

Many parents today mistakenly believe the answer to keeping their children in the faith begins and ends with a dynamic children's or youth ministry. For many the end-all is a youth ministry with exciting worship, relevant events, relational youth workers, personal mentoring, and a charismatic pastor. Sounds reasonable, right? But it doesn't work. Dr. Richard Ross, an expert in youth ministry of four decades, says,

> This model (of student ministry) has allowed us to maintain very strong participation for the sum total of two years of middle school, then we lose the first group on their way to high school, the next group when they get their driver's license, and the last group in the spring of their senior year. The fact that most now sleep off hangovers on Sunday mornings in the dorms suggests our model, though well intentioned, has generally been a failed experiment. Scripture, research, and observation by seasoned youth leaders suggest it is time for a new model.[90]

Our current model of educational formation in church isn't producing lasting disciples even if we get a sharper pastor, newer gimmicks, a better youth band, more volunteers, a bigger budget, or even our own youth building. Unfortunately pastors who work with students today are gauged by their coolness factor and their ability to entertain and act as kid magnet. What if our ministries had no lights, no shows, no gimmicks, no Christian celebrities, no budget, but had prayerful and humble leaders? What if prayer was primary, Scripture was central, and sharing one's faith was the norm? What if moms and dads were teaching the Word at home, living daily as attractive models to follow? What if these parents understood that, biblically, it's not the job of a professional pastor to disciple their children for them?

I've been a student pastor for twenty years. If someone asked me what is the one thing I want to accomplish in my ministry, the answer would be easy. My goal is to resource, train, and involve parents so that they begin to open the Scriptures at home and pray with their children. I want parents to see their role as the most significant and influential in their God-given task to disciple their children.

Parents must take ownership of the responsibility to be the disciplers to their child. Pastors want to help and support parents, but when pastors try to do it alone, we see two-thirds of students walk away from the church after high school.[91] Parent, take hold of your privilege.

You and I have seen both good and bad habits in families. Among the good I have found seven of the most impacting habits that I have seen families adopt. This list is in no way the top ten list of discipleship. These are simply seven habits I have seen working in spiritually growing families in my church, and I would encourage you to prayerfully consider. Some may be new for you, so I have briefly explained them. They are:

1. Family worship
2. Praying as a family
3. Serving as a family
4. Passage trips
5. Journaling
6. Journey days
7. Family dinnertime

## FAMILY WORSHIP

If a casual observer were to visit our homes, what practice would he or she see that is distinctly "Christian"? In many families today there is little noticeable difference between the home lives of Christians and the home lives of the unchurched. It should make us wonder what traditions and habits we are passing down to our children. It is my conviction that children need to see dad and mom leading in the study of God's Word, sincere in their prayer life, and faithfully pointing to eternity. The Christian home has lost its badge of distinction as many families no longer practice family worship in their homes. I believe family worship, or whatever you choose to call it (family night, breakfast with Daddy, etc.), is the best place for our children to learn how to worship firsthand. Many of the great pastors of days past were faithful to admonish parents of this incredible privilege to lead their children. Listen to the great pastors of old:

- "Every Christian family ought to be as it were a little church, consecrated to Christ . . . family education and order are some of the chief means of grace." —Jonathan Edwards (1703–1758)

- "The welfare and glory of both the Church and the State depend much on family government and duty. . . . If you desire reformation, do all you can to promote family religion." —Richard Baxter (1615–1691)

- "Masters of families . . . must be as prophets, priests, and kings in their own families; and as such they must keep up family-doctrine, family-worship, and family-discipline." —Matthew Henry (1662–1714)

- "Brethren, you are ordained of God to rule your own houses in His true fear, and according to His word. . . . And therefore I say, you must make [your family] partakers in reading, exhorting, and in making common prayers, which I would in every house were used once a day at least." —John Knox (1510–1572)

- "First, let us begin by emphatically declaring it is parents (fathers in particular) and not the church who are given the primary responsibility for calling the next generation to hope in God. The church serves a supplementary role." —Charles Haddon Spurgeon (1834–1892)

Today, many pastors are still preaching these same truths:

- Ligon Duncan says, "Start family worship as soon as possible, as soon as one is married, and continue it after children come along, no matter how young the children are. The point is not for the youngest children to be able to comprehend (or even to sit still during it!). The point is impress upon them, by paternal example the priority of God and his word in all of life."[92]

- John Piper says, "We discovered that the very earliest 'school' for worship is in the home—when we help a baby be quiet for just a moment while we ask God's blessing on our meal; when a toddler is sitting still to listen to a Bible story book; when a child is learning to pay attention to God's Word and to pray during family devotional times."[93]

- Providence Baptist Church's senior pastor, David Horner, my pastor, also faithfully teaches this, saying, "Churches cannot provide what families neglect."[94]

It is hard to deny the importance of family worship. The Bible emphasizes it. Faithful pastors preach about it. It is the parents' responsibility to do it.

So, what would family worship look like for parents like you and me? In short, it looks different for each of us. There is danger of becoming trapped in legalism or beginning to compare your family to other families. Here are some ideas to get you started in family worship:

- Start small. Don't be extreme by setting a standard of an hour each day for family worship. This will set you up for failure. Be realistic on what time and how much time works best for everyone.

- Stick with it. It might be awkward at first for everyone (even you), but it will get easier over time.

- Be realistic. When and how often should be determined by what works for your family and puts a win under your family's belt. Some families start with once a month or once a week, some do every weekend, and others do five days a week. Some families meet in the morning, some at night. Choose what works for you.

- Have a plan. It could be structured or very informal, based on a Bible-reading plan or working through spiritual issues or questions. At first you may read one verse and share a statement of what God has been teaching you then end by praying for protection and blessing for your family. Some families have musical talent. Many young children love singing Bible songs), although my family is not one of those, so we don't incorporate music. Some families memorize a verse together.

- Give it time. Develop a plan for a few weeks, then evaluate later to determine if you need to make some minor tweaks or create a new plan entirely. Don't worry, God will honor your efforts. He will finish His work.

- Make it interactive. It would be wise if it weren't a one-sided sermon. Make sure that your goal isn't to simply scold your kids. This is a time to focus on the Lord and His Word, not on our kids' failures and weaknesses.

- Don't overwhelm them. Make the worship time inviting and short enough leaving your children wanting for more. Then increase the length and depth as everyone gets more comfortable.

- Be transparent. Be honest. Be open. Your children know you; so don't try to fool them. If you don't know what to say, then tell them so. In those moments, tell them that you are doing this because that is what the Bible tells us to do, and you are all learning this together.

One final word of advice: get to know parents who already have a set plan for family worship. Ask them questions. Learn from them, but understand that just because something works for their family doesn't mean it will work for yours. The specifics of family worship are not spelled out in the Bible, but it is very clear that it is our responsibility and privilege as parents. I also encourage you to use the Bible as your curriculum. There is so much confusion about which curriculum works with which age and whether or not your kids will like it. You can avoid these curriculum worries simply by going to the Bible. If you are searching for a Bible-reading plan, visit www.lastingdivergence.com and look for the "John Newton Challenge."

## Praying as a Family

I have a friend who decided when his boys were young to pray God's blessing on them each time they left the house.

He did this for years almost without exception. One day his son was getting ready to return to college and said, "Dad, aren't you going to pray for me before I leave?" This is the kind of legacy I hope to leave. I hope to make an impression for the Lord on my children and on their children and on their children. We aim much too low when our goal is for a legacy of temporal things. It's time to understand the eternal impact we can have on generations through prayer.

Your child's bedtime is a natural time for prayer. However, as our children grow up, this habit often gets pushed aside. Dinnertime is another natural moment for prayer, but many families hunger for the meatloaf more than they hunger and thirst for prayer. Bedtime and dinnertime along with breakfast and even driving in the car together are all natural times to pray. Take hold of these natural opportunities. What do you pray for? Make a list of prayer needs and post it where your children can watch in amazement as God faithfully answers your prayers.

Popular Christian author and speaker Nancy Leigh DeMoss wrote about the impact of her dad's prayer times:

"Daily devotions" was not something my parents forced on us, but the influence of my dad's example and training in this area was profound. Although he has been with the Lord since 1979, the image of a dad on his knees before the Lord (I don't know how many kneeling pads he wore out over the years) is indelibly etched on my mind and in my heart.[95]

There is power when our children see us pray. There is power when we pray together. There is power in prayer.

## SERVING AS A FAMILY

The Bride of Christ, the church, is beautiful. I hope you have found joy by serving the Bride and her eternal work. So many families are tempted to give their lives for things that are fleeting. I am saddened to see the families who give countless hours toward Little League, Tae Kwon Do, soccer, band, ballet, plays, Scouts, and more, who say later that they have no time to serve the Lord in the church. These aren't bad things in and of themselves, but wouldn't it make sense that we would serve the Bride of Christ at least with equal time and equal zeal?

A few years ago, Search Institute released a study on the major church denominations in the U.S. that revealed roughly two-thirds of young people rarely or never serve the church with their families through missions or by caring for other families.[96] In subsequent research they found that the top four habits to successfully pass faith on to your kids were: faith conversations with mom, faith conversations with dad, Bible reading and prayer with parents, and serving together as a family.[97] Family service is both important and rare. At our church many families go on mission trips together, dads bring along their sons for church projects, and moms teach Vacation Bible School with their daughters. The opportunities are all around. We just have to look for them and be intentional.

## PASSAGE TRIPS

In Namibia, a boy is not a man until he has killed an animal. In Kampuchea, Cambodia, girls are secluded at the onset of puberty for a long period of time, and when they return they are adult women, ready for marriage. In Borneo, a boy is left alone in the wilderness to hunt and become a man. Jewish children have Bar Mitzvahs and Bat Mitzvahs to mark their becoming adults. Rites of passage are common in almost every culture, and one sociologist says, "If boys have no rituals, they will invent some." Many of these invented rituals result in gang initiations, fraternity hazing, or sexual accomplishments.[98] The purpose of what we call "Passage Trips" is to help our children understand that they are transitioning to adulthood before God, ready to own their own faith and ready to live for Christ.

Two years ago, my wife took our daughter, Sara, to Atlanta for her Passage Trip. Last year, my son William and I spent four days at Snowshoe, West Virginia, for his Passage Trip. These trips serve as a visible reminder to our children that they are valued and loved. They demonstrate to our children that that we will be there to guide them safely through the often-turbulent teen years.

We encourage every family in our ministry to plan a Passage Trip. Some of our families have had extravagant trips, while others have planned with simplicity in mind. The cost of the trip is never the point. The students in our ministry love these trips and become increasingly excited as they get closer because they do a large portion of the dreaming, research, and planning for the trip. This level of involvement involves them early and sets this trip apart from any they have ever been a part of before. After the trip, things at home should be different; expectations should be raised.

Blake Hickman, Providence's middle school pastor, lays out four components to a Passage Trip and the seventh-grade year in our ministry we call Passage 7:

- It should be challenging. This is an experience that stretches both parent and child, not an experience that can be done in your sleep.

- It should be memorable. One that you look back on twenty years from now as a memory that helped strengthen your relationship.

- It should be biblical. This is an experience that is foundational in the spiritual development of you and your child. It will help them be better able to tackle the difficult life challenges that await them in the upcoming years.

- It should be relational. We hope it is a good time. It is designed to create an opportunity for you and your student to spend time together planning an experience that is new, memorable, foundational, and fun.

During this trip most parents and children have fun doing something they have never done before. The trips for boys are often more adventurous: hunting, skiing, or hiking. The trips for girls are also adventurous as they involve travel, meaningful conversation, shopping, and trying new food. During this trip, conversations are intentional. They often cover sex and purity, responsibility and integrity, modesty and pornography, and biblical manhood and biblical womanhood. We also encourage parents to give their children a journal they have written in throughout the previous year.

## JOURNALING

I have never considered myself a writer, yet I have written four books in my life. Two have been published, like the one you are holding. Two never will be. Yesterday, I began my fifth book, which will never be published either. The three unpublished books were written for my three children: Sara, William, and Tyler. These three books are journals and by far have brought me the greatest joy. In them, I share my memories, hopes for them, prayers for them, important life lessons, foundational Scriptures, and above all what it means to follow Christ.

At Providence we encourage the parents of our seventh graders to journal during the year before their Passage Trip. We have a parent meeting early in the year, and we hand out leather journals full of blank parchment paper that, once filled, will serve as a lifelong reminder of what each of us truly value.

I remember asking one dad at my church how the journaling was going. He said he hadn't written a word because he didn't know what to write. I suggested that he start with his memory of bringing his precious little girl home from the hospital. The next week, I saw his wife and asked her if he had written anything yet and found out he still hadn't.

But before I could ask why, she told me that it was because now he breaks down in tears every time he tries to express his love, memories, and dreams to his daughter. This dad did finish his daughter's journal, and I can promise you that she will cherish that journal for a lifetime.

## JOURNEY DAYS

The journey is the path to biblical manhood and womanhood, becoming the man or woman of God your child is created to be. The road to biblical manhood and womanhood is not always an easy one, but it is an extremely important one, *especially today*. I regularly counsel parents who are concerned about the femininity of their sons, homosexual tendencies with sons and daughters, and the ever-blurring lines of masculinity and femininity. If biblical manhood and womanhood isn't on your radar as a parent, it better get there quickly. There is a logic going around young people to "try everything" before they decide if they are gay or straight. Our children must decide if the biblical framework is relevant for today or not, and they need their parents to guide them through those questions. Is your child on the right course as a young man or young woman? Consider these questions:

- Who is a biblical man or a biblical woman?
- What is biblical masculinity and femininity?
- How does a boy become a man?
- How does a girl become a woman?
- What are the roles within Christian marriage?

- What roles do men and women play at home, church, and society?
- Are they prepared to lead a family of their own?

Many young people are lost concerning the definition of manhood and womanhood, and they need affirmation. They need a guide on their journey. Parent, that guide is you. They need your leadership shaping their life, character, and purpose. They need your help discovering God's vision for their life, and this affirmation must come from you. Your student needs you to provide direction from God's Word on the characteristics of a godly man and a godly woman and how they become one.

Who do you think are the major influencers in your son's or daughter's life? Is it a grandparent, a coach, a neighbor, an uncle or aunt, a pastor, or a friend? A Journey Day is an unforgettable day of affirmation and initiation for your child created by you, the parent. It also involves these major influencers in your child's life who may help answer some of the above questions. These influencers would be used on this day to speak truth into your son's or daughter's lives concerning biblical manhood and womanhood.

The Journey begins when you start planning for the event months in advance. At our church a Journey Day could be a sweet sixteen party or a significant event celebrating an accomplishment such as memorizing a book of the Bible, completing a service project, running a half marathon, rebuilding an engine, or climbing a difficult mountain. Next, get others involved. Find those key influencers and get them involved on the day that you choose. Talk to them about what part they will play and specific questions they will answer. For example, a grandmother may take her granddaughter to breakfast in the morning and talk about wisdom, then a mentor from church may take her to get a pedicure and talk about modesty, and so on. Ideally, each person would give your child a small gift as a reminder of the message they shared. Then plan an event or ceremony to conclude the day. Invite over your child's friends to be at the house when your child returns. Have some food and fun, but make sure the parents, especially the dad, affirms and challenges your son or daughter in front of everyone to treasure Christ. Close with your child showing the gifts he or she received and sharing with the group what he or she learned on the Journey Day. For additional resources on Journey Days and Passage Trips, see the suggested books in the endnotes.[99]

## FAMILY DINNERTIME

It's a fact that when families eat dinner together, kids are less likely to drink, smoke, use drugs, have an eating disorder, get depressed, consider suicide, fail a school, or have sex.[100]   All of this is accomplished through conversation over a casserole. An important article in *TIME* magazine says that teens are hungry for dinnertime with the family. Miriam Weinstein says:

> We've sold ourselves on the idea that teenagers are obviously sick of their families, that they're bonded to their

peer group. We've taken it to an extreme. We've taken it to mean that a teenager has no need for his family. And that's just not true. . . . Parents may be undervaluing themselves when they conclude that sending kids off to every conceivable extracurricular activity is a better use of time than an hour spent around a table, just talking to Mom and Dad.[101]

David Lynn, a thirty-year veteran of youth ministry and author of more than thirty-five books, emphatically states we must "strive for five," which means to eat "a meal together without interruptions (no television, video games, phone, etc.) at least five times a week."[102]  The research is clear that family mealtime five to seven days a week is that important.[103] Dinnertime gets harder to manage the older our children get, but it just may become even more critical. This habit, though it sounds simplistic, will harvest incredible results for your family.

## WHERE DO I START?

In 1994, Deborah Kemp stopped to fill her car with gas. As she left to pay the attendant, someone jumped in her car to steal it. Deborah fought back. The thirty-four-year-old woman was dragged for several blocks as she clung to the steering wheel. Kemp eventually pulled the man from the moving car and beat him with an anti-theft device until he begged her to stop. When police arrived on the scene, they determined that Deborah had two bloody knees while the thief had two broken legs and numerous head injuries.

Why did Deborah Kemp value her car that much? She didn't. Her six-year-old daughter Ashleye was in the back-seat.[104]

How far would you go to protect the lives of your children? How far would you go to look after their eternal souls? Remember Christ's warning, "The thief comes only to steal and kill and destroy" (John 10:10). We are facing a thief and enemy who is much more evil and much more crafty than Deborah's would-be robber. Will we put the same passion into fighting off our thief that Deborah put into fighting off hers? There are a lot of incredible habits and traditions mentioned in this chapter, but it isn't just about the everyday habits. It's ultimately about protecting our children's souls from our enemy.

You may read the above habits, knowing of other equally meaningful discipleship ideas as well, then you wonder where to start. I have to agree with previous quotes from pastors who are wiser than me that stress the importance of family worship. There is no more vital family habit than to spend time reading the Word and praying together. I would start with family worship. I would then ask myself which of the other ideas stir me. Is there one that jumps out, that connects to you on a deeper level? That may be the next direction to take. Be intentional. Be focused. But remember: these habits are simply parents' tools that God can use. I pray He uses these habits and your very lives as you care for the eternal souls of those in your home.

=== 8 ===

# A PARENT'S ROLE: A CALL TO FATHERS

See if you recognize these famous last words:

- "Let's roll." (Todd Beamer, passenger on United Flight 93, September 11, 2001.)

- "It's very beautiful over there." (Thomas Edison, spoken to his wife as he lapsed in and out of consciousness)

- "I've always loved my wife, my children, and my grand-children, and I've always loved my country. I want to go. God, take me." (Dwight D. Eisenhower)

- "Is everyone else alright?" (Robert F. Kennedy, whispered to his wife directly after he was shot and seconds before he fell into a coma)

- "Be sure to play 'Blessed Lord' tonight—play it real pretty." (Martin Luther King Jr.)

- "I am just going. Have me decently buried and do not

let my body be into a vault in less than two days after I am dead. Do you understand me? . . . 'Tis well. I die hard, but I am not afraid to go." (George Washington, who had a fear of being buried alive)

- "Go therefore and make disciples of all nations, baptizing them in the name of the Father and of the Son and of the Holy Spirit, teaching them to observe all that I have commanded you. And behold, I am with you always, to the end of the age." (Jesus' final words before He ascended, also called the Great Commission, in Matthew 28:19–20)

Often the last things people say are the most important. When our kids are heading out the door, usually we remember we have one last thing to mention. We place the words of the Great Commission on the walls of our churches and underline them in our Bibles. Many people save their best thoughts for last.

Can you remember the famous last words of the Old Testament? Think for a moment of the significance of the Old Testament as it prepared for the Messiah, taught the Law, and contained so many incredible stories of our God. It ends with the book of Malachi. I rarely read or ever hear about studies from Malachi, but it contains a closing verse that I can't get out of my head. Perhaps this last verse isn't as much of a closing as it is an opening. The famous last words of the Old Testament are: "And he will turn the hearts of fathers to their children and the hearts of children to their fathers, lest I come and strike the land with a decree of utter destruction" (Malachi 4:6). Of all of the ways that the Old Testament could have closed, notice how with laser accuracy it zeros in on one particular group—fathers. God could have mentioned social problems, horrific sins of the day, five tips for biblical living, or even the Ten Commandments, but He closes the Old Testament by drawing attention to the importance of the heart of the father. Rick Johnson, founder of Better Dads says, "I don't think it's a coincidence that the last words God spoke to His people at the end of the Old Testament—His last words for four hundred years—were on the importance of fathering."[105] Why? I believe it is more than an abrupt or odd ending. I believe it is a call to fathers. A call we must hear today.

## SHAPING ETERNITY—A FATHER'S GREATEST CALLING

My eighth-grade year was difficult for me. I might have never recovered from that year had my dad not been there to play his God-given role as a father. I had always played sports. I had a fire in me that made every competition a life-or-death matter. I had to win, but there was a problem. My friends were growing rapidly, and I was not. Try to visualize this if you can. I weighed a whopping sixty-five pounds and was playing junior high football against giant boys who weighed two hundred or more pounds. My football career didn't last long, and basketball was also out of the question. As my friends grew to be six feet or taller, I was nowhere close. So, my dad suggested that I try out for the wrestling team so that I could compete against guys my size. It was the perfect fit.

After my very first wrestling tournament, a man sat down beside me and said, "Did you know there has never been a wrestler from the state of Georgia who has won a collegiate national championship?" That is all I remember this stranger saying. On the way home that night I asked my dad if he knew about this piece of news. He said, "Son, that is horrible for our state, but I have no doubt in my mind whatsoever that if you set your mind to it, you will be the first." Because my dad believed in me I went straight to my room and wrote my new goal on an index card and put it on my mirror. "I will become the first wrestler from the state of Georgia to win a college national championship."

Because my dad was there, I avoided many of the temptations that my friends fell prey to. Because he was there, I continued wrestling, which led me to meet Christ through a teammate. Because of my dad, Georgia wrestling history is different because my father's prophecy came true when I won the national championship in 1988.

Being in ministry where I see fatherless children rips my heart out. Most children are fatherless because their father figure is missing in action due to divorce, separation, never marrying his partner, or possibly death. Many other children are essentially fatherless because dad is consumed at work both outside and inside the home leaving only a few hours a month to spend with his children. However, I have realized that there is another type of situation, one less noticed but just as common—spiritual fatherlessness.

This dad lives at home, provides financially for his family, coaches his child's team, even drops his kids off at school or Bible study and might even attend church, but he isn't purposeful in leading his family spiritually. I can think of many Christ-honoring moms who bring their children to church and sit alone in the service because their husbands do not come to church. This dad may be a moral man, a respectable person, and a hard worker, but he never prays with his child, never talks about God, thus neglecting his calling to lead his family spiritually. This type of father-lessness, especially for young boys, often results in children who walk away from their faith as they follow their dad's footsteps. These children add it up and may conclude, "If Christ isn't that important to my dad, then I can leave Him out of my life as well."

God has given dads an unequalled role. I might not be writing this book, raising a Christian family, or serving in ministry if it weren't for my dad. Dads are that important. So, dad, let me share my heart with you, from one dad to another. Here are a few things I have learned from the pages of Scripture and the lessons of life:

## 1. Dad, think about your unparalleled influence.

You don't need to talk to a Ph.D. or spend a million on research to understand the importance of dads. Just look at the headlines of the newspaper and you'll see that this is a critical area of attack:

- Sixty-three percent of youth suicides are from fatherless homes.[106]
- Ninety percent of all homeless and runaway children grew up in fatherless homes.[107]
- Eighty-five percent of all children who exhibit behavioral disorders are from fatherless homes.[108]
- Eighty percent of rapists were raised in fatherless homes.[109]
- Seventy-one percent of all high school dropouts come from fatherless homes.[110]
- Seventy-five percent of all adolescent patients in chemical abuse centers are from fatherless homes.[111]
- Seventy percent of juveniles in state-operated institutions come from fatherless homes.[112]
- Eighty-five percent of all youths sitting in prisons grew up in a fatherless home.[113]

According to Wade Horn of the National Fatherhood Initiative, we must do something to reverse the trend or within a decade our society may never recover.[114] Before you go into statistical overload, here's a short recap of why dads are so important. Fatherless children are:

- five times more likely to commit suicide;
- thirty-two times more likely to run away;
- twenty times more likely to have behavioral disorders;
- fourteen times more likely to commit rape (this applies to boys of course);
- nine times more likely to drop out of high school;

- ten times more likely to abuse chemical substances;
- nine times more likely to end up in a state-operated institution; and
- twenty times more likely to end up in prison.

In fact, the largest factor in predicting whether a child will graduate from high school, attend college, become involved in crime or drugs, or get pregnant before age eighteen is the presence (or absence) of a father in the child's life. Not the quality of your child's church or school. Not if the child lives in the inner city with daily drive-by shootings. Not your education, the size of your house, or the amount of your paycheck. The main determining factor for these statistics is if dad is there.

You and I have seen firsthand why dads are crucial. John Stonestreet with Summit Ministries discussed the alarming number of children who walk away from the faith. He said, "In my experience, 80 percent of those who walk away do so because of family trauma. And 80 percent of that trauma is specifically tied to their fathers."[115] The presence or absence of dad drastically affects a child's intellectual development, key relationships, self-image, future plans, and even his or her view of God. A dad's influence is unparalleled.

## 2. Dad, your modeling is irreplaceable.

The power of the example of a dad's life is unequalled. Whether you have boys or girls, you are teaching your children lifelong lessons. Rick Johnson talks to dads, saying,

"You are so important that you are nearly irreplaceable in the lives of your children—especially your son. Fatherhood is a privilege given by God, and with that privilege comes the power to impact lives."[116]

- Every daughter looks to her dad for what she will one day look for in a husband. Michael Harris, author of *What a Daughter Needs from Her Dad*, says, "Your role in your daughter's life will have profound, lifelong effects on her. You will shape—for good or for ill—her ideas about her husband."[117]

- Every son learns from dad what a masculine man looks like in a feminized culture. Steve Farrar gives a very wise warning: "But if you let your wife become the primary mentors of your sons, one of two things will happen. They will grow up to be feminized men or they will grow up to be angry men."[118] This is why I encourage single moms to engage a godly man at her church in helping disciple her son.

- Every daughter gains confidence when her father loves her. When a dad cherishes, adores, and protects his daughter, she has no reason to seek another man's affection or go outside a biblical framework to feel loved. James Dobson says, "Long before a girl finds her first real boyfriend or falls in love, her attitude toward men has been shaped quietly by her father. Why? Because the father-daughter relationship sets the stage for all future romantic involvements. If a young woman's father rejects her, she'll spend her life trying to find a man who can meet the needs he never fulfilled in her heart."[119]

Dad, whether you have a son or daughter, your modeling is critically important. John Angell James says, "As you wish your instructions and admonitions to your family to be successful, enforce them by the power of a holy example."[120] Your model and example are irreplaceable.

### 3. Dad, your calling is to lead your family spiritually.

Isn't there more to life than bringing home the bacon? I know that providing for my family is part of my role as a dad, and I am glad to take care of them. However, my paycheck can't be my greatest gift to my family. Paychecks don't make a man and don't define a dad. What will we pass on to our son or daughter that equips them for life and for eternity? What will we pass on to them that is truly enduring?

The culture places the highest value on financially leading our families, so much that workaholic dads are accepted and sometimes praised. Dads who work fifty to sixty hours a week or are out of town five out of seven days a week are too commonplace. A survey of five hundred men found that dads believe they have to neglect their children due to their demanding work schedules. The survey also found that many dads have to work nights, weekends, and holidays causing them to not be able to attend school plays, be present for special events, or even personally buy birthday presents for their children.[121] Dads are busier than ever in an effort to provide for their family.

The Bible puts high value on work and supporting a family. For instance, 1 Timothy 5:8 says, "If anyone does not provide for his relatives, and especially for members of his household, he has denied the faith and is worse than an unbeliever." However, while the Bible puts a high value on providing for physical needs, it places the highest value on meeting spiritual needs. It is clear that your marriage is of utmost importance as it is a picture of Christ and the church. The best gift you can give your children is a home founded on Christ-honoring marriage. The Bible is also clear about your privilege to teach your children. We have covered many verses that lay out the roles that parents, especially dads, have in spiritually leading their family and teaching their children. Here is a reminder:

- "The father makes known to the children your faithfulness" (Isaiah 38:19).

- "Fathers, do not provoke your children to anger, but bring them up in the discipline and instruction of the Lord" (Ephesians 6:4).

- "He will go before him in the spirit and power of Elijah, to turn the hearts of the fathers to the children" (Luke 1:17).

- "He commanded our fathers to teach to their children, that the next generation might know them, the children yet unborn, and arise and tell them to their children" (Psalm 78:5–6).

Dads, you have an apparent privilege to teach your children the truths of God. Don't miss out on the greatest blessing of your life.

## 4. Dad, you must decide what legacy you will leave.

What will our children and grandchildren have when we are gone? This may be an uncomfortable thought, but it is one we must consider. I don't want my children to have just a big inheritance or a large piece of land. While these things are admirable, I want my legacy to be more than just the here and now. And I'm not the only one.

Every dad has a dream for his child—passion, a hope. Most often this aspiration begins easily enough and appears noble and worthy of pursuit. But as our children grow older these pursuits can take on a life of their own: education and acceptance into a prestigious university, athletic accomplishments that will someday lead to a scholarship or professional career, musical skills that will amaze people, or a strategic path that leads to a high-paying career. Even in the middle of these pursuits, most Christian parents would say, "Sure, it is very important that our kids love God, the church, and the Bible." All the while our actions, our time, and our spending patterns demonstrate to our children and others what we actually value.

So dad, what is your dream for your child? What are you most passionate about for your children? Hold this passion up against eternity and answer these questions: Which is more real? More lasting? Most capable of carrying your child from death to life? Those are the dreams we must pursue.

John Piper writes, "Life is wasted when we do not live all of life for the glory of God. And I do mean all of life. It is all for His glory."[122] Our children and their children after them will only gain Christ when they observe that life isn't about them being center stage. Our lives are to be spent in joy making much about Christ. Then and only then will our legacy last forever and ever and ever.

### 5. Dad, you are fighting a battle for your children and generations to come.

Where was Adam when Eve was being tempted? Look at Genesis 3:6: "So when the woman saw that the tree was good for food, and that it was a delight to the eyes, and that the tree was to be desired to make one wise, she took of its fruit and ate, and she also gave some to her husband *who was with her*, and he ate" (emphasis mine). He was with her! What should Adam have done when he saw Eve being tempted? Maybe a better question is: What should he have done to the serpent? I'd like to think it would involve the sharp end of a shovel. Because Adam didn't stand up for his family, many generations later his descendant would have to pay a great price to defeat Satan. This is explained in Genesis 3:15, which prophesies that Jesus would crush the serpent. Do you battle sin? Do you battle a particular sin? Are there sins that have cursed your family for generations? Will you leave this battle for your son or grandson or daughters or granddaughters to fight, or will you fight it now? John Owen says, "Be killing sin or it will be killing you."[123]

There is a battle going on for the souls of our children and we cannot sit by passively to wait and see how it turns out. Our children are fighting this same battle and looking to us, their fathers, to find direction. John 10:10 reminds us of a deadly adversary: "The thief comes only to steal and kill and destroy. I came that they may have life and have it abundantly." We must remember that there is a battle going on today, an enemy who wants to destroy us and a God who is all-powerful. Fight for your children. Never give up. Never give up. Never give up.

## 6. Dad, you can have a fresh start today.

I hope you feel the heart of a warrior beating within your chest. I believe God has placed a spirit to fight within every father who desires to protect those who have been placed within his care. I hope you recognize the incredible privilege you have each time you walk in the door from work. You may feel you have waited too late or that you have made too many mistakes. Perhaps you are paralyzed by guilt. Whatever your fear is, God's grace will overcome it. It is never too late for a new beginning.

The Bible is full of stories of men who turned their lives around. Abraham's lies, Moses' murder, David's adultery and murder, Jonah's running from God, Peter's denials, and Paul's hatred of Christ—they were all overcome for these men who changed history. That's not bad company to be in. God received much glory through the lives of these imperfect men, and their influence continues to this day. It isn't too late. God created you with incredible plans in mind. He sent His Son to die for your sins before you ever knew of your need, and His Spirit intercedes daily for you. He cares more about your children than even you do, so He will give wisdom when you ask, strength when you need it, and hope when you doubt. Today He will give you a fresh start and the grace you need to change. Go to Him. He never fails.

## A New Vision

I often hear dads say, "Steve, I agree with what you are saying, and I wish I had more time to do some of the things you are talking about, but my job . . ." This is where I usually cut them off. God has given a job description to us, and there is no escape clause even for dads who work a certain number of hours. You see, our career isn't really our job. Our career puts food on the table and keeps the lights on so that we can do our real job. Our real job is laid out clearly in the Word. In case you don't have this job description, you may want to print it and keep it in front of you.

## A Job Description for Dad

**Love your Lord with everything you've got.**

Matthew 22:37–38 says, "You shall love the Lord your God with all your heart and with all your soul and with all your mind. This is the great and first commandment." If Jesus said that this is the most important thing we can do, then it is also the most important thing a dad can do.

**Love and lead your bride.**

Ephesians 5:25 says, "Husbands, love your wives, as Christ loved the church and gave himself up for her." The message is to serve your bride just as Christ served His Bride, the church, to the point that He laid down His life for her.

**Love and teach your children.**

Ephesians 6:4 says, "Fathers, do not provoke your children to anger, but bring them up in the discipline and instruction of the Lord." This verse sums up the biblical mandate for dads. Dads must lead the effort to give their children an eternal perspective, show them their need for Christ, and continually point them to the Savior.

## A Call to Fathers

In the 1400s, the Muslim Ottoman Empire was forcibly expanding and Christianity was being pushed out of the

Middle East. As Amurath I, ruler of the Muslim Empire, conquered more lands he instructed his troops to take the smartest and strongest from the Christian families held as captives to become an elite group known as the Janizaries. Many Christian families voluntarily gave over their sons, seeing it as a scholarship with guaranteed food and education, ignoring the fanatical Muslim doctrine their sons were being immersed into. In 1453, the Muslim Ottoman army attacked Constantinople, the seat of the Eastern Church. They besieged the city with one hundred thousand troops, while Christian Constantinople could only muster seven thousand to try to hold off the assault. As the few remaining troops held off the Muslim attack, screams were heard all over the city. The Muslim army had unleashed the Janizaries. Their young voices rang out throughout the city as they didn't understand or didn't care that they were slaughtering their own families. They were brutal. They were effective. And Constantinople fell that day.[124]

Our sons and daughters will be trained. They will fight for something. Will you be the one training them?

You may see what is at stake and know that you must train your children, but still wonder where to start. Great question. Important question. Start with prayer. Maybe go to lunch with a dad who meets the above job description and ask him questions. Be open with your wife about your concerns, fears, failures, hopes, dreams, and vision. Have a family meeting and ask your family to help you evaluate (I'm sure they will be honest). If necessary, ask for forgiveness. I'm not sure which of these things you need to do because they are often different for each of us. Just take one step toward your biblical assignment and you will find God doing the work: "For it is God who works in you, both to will and to work for his good pleasure" (Philippians 2:13). God will meet you. He will guide. He will be the Father you need, as you become the father they need.

# A Parent's Need: Grace for a Prodigal

When I was ten years old, I had enough of my parents' demanding control and decided that it was time for me to live by my own set of rules. I had been camping a few times, obviously had watched many Tom Sawyer and Huck Finn reruns, so I knew I was prepared for the challenges ahead. Looking back, I now see that one of my older cousins implanted the idea of running away in my head. Nevertheless, I made up my mind that I was moving out, and gave my dad the news. He called my bluff by saying he understood and would help me pack my bags, so I was off. I had my first taste of freedom.

The first hour or two wasn't that bad as I sat in the woods near my house watching to see how my family was coping with the harrowing loss. Then my uncle Hoss showed up. He had been away on a trip, and since he had no children of his own, he would bring gifts to my brother, my sister, and me. On this day he brought my brother and me the best gift ever—a mini-motorcycle. I remember watching my uncle, my dad, and my brother unloading the new off-road dirt bike from his truck. Then I had to sit and watch my brother drive it for hours without having to take any turns with me. Occasionally, my dad and uncle could be overheard saying how badly they wished I hadn't run away and how much fun I could have been having.

I crawled up on my belly as close as I could get to them. When I couldn't take it any longer I did what any prideful young boy would do—I started yelling and crying to fake an injury. The only honorable way I could return home was to seek medical treatment. After receiving the necessary treatment, my dad sent me to my room and told me I could ride the bike the next day. For the rest of the day, my brother rode it by my bedroom window at least ten thousand times, and I never ran away again.

Children have the ability to bring the greatest joy and the greatest heartache. There are days when we watch our children with amazement. When my children were younger and unable to communicate fully, I would often find myself wondering just what might be going through their little heads. Then there were hard times when a greater concern possessed me as I wondered what was going on in their hearts. I would find myself praying for them and asking God to capture their hearts, as I watched them struggle with sins like their daddy. I would be consumed with a heavy burden when I considered what the Scriptures said about the sinful hearts of my three precious children.

I know the burden of caring for our children's hearts. Through the years, I have observed numerous attempts by parents to guard, protect, and shelter their children from this inward battle as well as the cruel, sin-sick world we live in. These fears have prompted some parents to embrace various forms of legalism as their hope and security. Other parents set up harsh rules and severe consequences, hoping that they might quarantine their children as a way of protection. Yet in all of this, I have watched some of these children rebel and become prodigals.

On the other hand, I have also seen many parents who have (in my opinion) done everything by the book. These parents focused on relationships and modeled Christ daily for their children, yet in the end some of their children rebelled and became prodigals. The same could be said of the first two people God placed on earth. I often remind parents that God placed Adam and Eve in an incredibly "safe" environment. The problem they faced was a matter of the heart, not external influences. There were no drugs, gangs, Internet porn, vulgar TV shows, or wrong crowds. But somehow, even in an environment I would cherish to place my three children in, Adam and Eve found sin. Why? It was a heart issue, just as ultimately is the case of every prodigal.

The most famous story of a prodigal is found in Luke 15. In the parable of the prodigal son, a young man demands his inheritance from his dad, wastes it on wild living, and returns in shame, only to find his father running toward him, accepting and forgiving him. An often-overlooked detail of the story is that when the son demanded his inheritance, his father wrote the check! Why would he give over so much money to a selfish son he knew he could not trust? I think he wrote the check for two reasons. First, he had likely exhausted all other options. He had come to know the hardness of his son's heart and had to give him over to God. Only the parent of a prodigal knows what this dad had to be feeling when he had run out of ideas. Secondly, this dad had an eternal perspective. He was willing to let go of the temporal—half of all he owned—giving his son over to the Lord and allowing him to learn the hard lessons of life, hoping his son's heart would be won back. Even though he knew his son would blow it all, hope remained that giving up so much would be worth it if his son found Christ. He was willing to sacrifice the temporal for the eternal. In our most difficult days of parenting we can't forget that God inspired Luke to include this parable for our benefit. John Angell James wrote:

> None, not even you, are too bad to be reclaimed. ...What prodigal can wander further, sink lower, or seem more out of the way of recovery, or more remote from the region of hope—than he was? Yet he was restored! And why was the parable spoken, and why was it written—but to encourage hope, in cases seemingly the most deplorable and abandoned?[125]

This parable is in the Bible to give us a picture of our sin and our need for God's grace. It is included so you and I will have hope. It is written so you and I will be reminded to be ready to run to our wayward child when God perfectly answers our tearful prayers. One pastor said:

Read this parable slowly and carefully and absorb its details and grandeur. Charles Dickens, the great English author, has called it "the greatest story ever told." Some say it is the finest short story in literature. Another poet, Robert Bridges, has judged it as a "flawless piece of art." Small wonder that through the centuries, this story has inspired the pen of Rembrandt, the music of DeBussey, and the poetry of John Masefield. George Buttrick, one of the greatest preachers of recent past, has said that the story of the prodigal son captures "the essence of the Christian faith." This story sums the central message of the whole New Testament. It is the gospel in a nutshell.[126]

## WHO IS THE PRODIGAL?

Isaiah 53 is the most famous and vivid prophecy of the death of Christ. In verse 6, it also points out an alarming fact about ourselves: "All we like sheep have gone astray; we have turned—every one—to his own way." Romans 3:12 is another one of those smack-in-the-face verses that says, "All have turned aside; together they have become worthless; no one does good, not even one." Notice the words in the above verses: *we, everyone, all, no one, not even one,* which would include me and you. At church we sing "Come Thou Fount of Every Blessing," which tells me that I am "prone to wander, Lord I feel it; prone to leave the God I love."[127] The truth concerning the prodigal is that we all know him very personally. This rebel is seen in the mirror each morning as we reach for our toothbrush. The truth of God's Word tells us that we are all prodigals. In other words, the spoiled younger son who disrespected his father and wasted his inheritance on a party lifestyle . . . that guy is me. The rich young ruler who would rather hold on to the short-lived possessions instead of the far-surpassing riches found in Christ...that guy is me. Those mean, judgmental, self-righteous Pharisees who sized themselves up by the failures of others rather than righteousness of Christ...me. When on the road to Gethsemane, James and John argue over who is more important, when Jesus had just taken the low place to embrace the towel over the title...my heart is revealed. I know the prodigal heart, because I am a prodigal. We all are.

When we think about our rebellious child, we forget the ground we have in common with the prodigal. We forget that the same grace the rebel needs to return to Christ is the same grace that we need to daily reflect a holy God. We are no better; we all need God's unmerited grace. We are all prodigals. We all need grace. These facts must change the way we think about parenting and the way we extend grace to our prodigal child.

## An Outpouring of Grace

In the parable of the prodigal son, notice how the father responds to the rebel. He runs to him. He embraces him. He celebrates. How does God, our Father, respond to us, the prodigals? He delights to show us grace. At the most shameful point of our sinful rebellion, He shows us grace, and He doesn't stop there. He continues to show us grace every day. The Bible says:

- "You, our God, have punished us less than our iniquities deserved and have given us such a remnant as this" (Ezra 9:13).

- "Who is a God like you, pardoning iniquity and passing over transgression for the remnant of his inheritance? He does not retain his anger forever, because he delights in steadfast love. He will again have compassion on us; he will tread our iniquities underfoot. You will cast all our sins into the depths of the sea" (Micah 7:18–19).

- "The LORD is merciful and gracious, slow to anger and abounding in steadfast love. . . . He does not deal with us according to our sins, nor repay us according to our iniquities. For as high as the heavens are above the earth, so great is his steadfast love toward those who fear him; as far as the east is from the west, so far does he remove our transgressions from us. *As a father shows compassion to his children,* so the LORD shows compassion to those who fear him" (Psalm 103:8, 10–13, emphasis mine).

Did you catch that? God shows us compassion in the same way a father is to show compassion to his children. Luke 6:36 commands the same thing, telling us to "be merciful, even as your Father is merciful." God, our Father, has shown us compassion, so we too are to show compassion to our enemies, our neighbors, our friends, our family, and our prodigal children.

Grace isn't ignoring and overlooking every sin of our prodigal; it is seeing his sin like God does. Grace is not helping your prodigal continue his or her sinful lifestyle or refusing to have the tough conversations. This grace is revealed in the cross, which reminds us that Jesus paid the price for our sin and the sins of our children. The cross shows us we deserve nothing but judgment and hell, but we, like our children, are saved only by grace. This grace understands that we don't get to claim the moral high ground, looking down on the poor sinners beneath us. We come to our children as sinners equally in need of a Savior. We confess our sin and ask forgiveness for where we have failed God and where we have failed them. We do all we can to keep the lines of communication open to share with our children the incredible Gospel of God's grace. When we gaze at the cross and see that it is all by grace and not by our merit, we see the Gospel as truly great. We also see that the Gospel is not just important for conversion, but is important each and every day of our lives. We openly admit that we are no better than any other sinner. We all need grace.

## Grace . . . Do you have it?

I love to ask people, "Have you seen evidences of God's grace in your life today?" I have. Think about it: Has God's grace been extended to you today? Has it? Can you articulate this effectively without seeming arrogant? Did you hear the birds singing when you woke this morning? Grace. Does someone love and care about you? Grace. Were you able to get out of bed on your own strength or read these words without help? Grace. Has Christ so captivated your heart today that your life isn't in ruin because of addiction to sin? Grace. Do you have a copy of God's Word sitting by your bed? Grace. Have you prayed to God today? Grace. Grace is all around us and, if we aren't careful, we can begin to take it for granted.

From the time our children are very small, we need to help them recognize their need for God's grace in their lives. Romans 2:4 says, "God's kindness is meant to lead you to repentance." So as we talk about the grace He so freely pours out, our children are led to the foot of the cross to find forgiveness. By modeling thankfulness for the grace we have received, we remind our children of their need for grace.

In our short, vaporous lives, so many things promise fulfillment, so many things seem lasting. They appear safe, satisfying, and even sustainable. They seem as delicious as the fruit that caused Eve to fall. A mentor of mine used to say that holding on to the things of the world is like trying to hold on to oil—you can't. Even when we know better as believers, we are constantly tempted to direct our children to find fulfillment in things that will not pass the test of eternity. Nothing shows an eternal perspective better than when we direct our children to see their need for a Savior and observe the outpouring of Christ's grace all around them. We need to be sensitive enough to see God's active grace in our lives and be grateful enough to share it as a way to pointing our children heavenward.

For that son who has not found his soul's fulfillment in Christ yet, for that daughter whose heart (for the time being) is seduced by the fleeting joys of this world, and even for our own prodigal hearts, we have hope. The Gospel of grace is our only hope for reconciliation with God, for eternal salvation, and for daily life change.

John Piper's son Abraham, a prodigal who has since returned, wrote an incredible article about reaching out to a wayward child. He writes about pointing the prodigal to Christ:

> This can't be over-stressed. It is the whole point. No strategy for reaching your son or daughter will have any lasting effect if the underlying goal isn't to help them know Jesus. It's not so that they will be good kids again; it's not so that they'll get their hair cut and start taking showers; it's not so that they'll like classical music instead of deathcore; it's not so that you can stop being embarrassed at your weekly Bible study; it's not so that they'll vote conservative again by the next election; it's not even so that you can sleep at night, knowing they're not going to hell. The only ultimate reason to pray for them, welcome them, plead with them, email them, eat with them, or take an interest in their interests is so that their eyes will be opened to Christ. And not only is he the only point—he's the only hope.[128]

Keep pointing your child to the Gospel of grace. Never stop. Christ's Gospel is our only hope.

## A GOSPEL OF GRACE

What is the ultimate aim of Christian parenting? What perspective must we keep in mind through the monotony of diapers, homework, soccer practice, endless to-do lists, and pleading for prodigals? Most of us would admit that our goal is to point our children to Christ. However, it isn't enough to slightly connect them to faith in hopes that they will benefit from good morals. Our biblical commission cannot be reduced to keeping them busy in Christian activities while they are under our roof. Step back and remember what is at stake. Ponder the great penalty of your child not knowing and loving Christ. None of us would wish that our children live as objects of God's wrath in this life or the age to come. Without Christ our children will be enslaved by the disgusting, destructive, and damning consequences of their sin. There is no other hope of salvation than the Gospel of God's grace in sending His Son to die for our sins and grant eternal life. Eternity is priority as a Christian parent. Now read this again one word at a time: *Eternity is priority as a Christian parent.* As David Michael, children's minister at Bethlehem Baptist Church in Minneapolis, Minnesota, says, eternal passion "is not our only aim but it is our ultimate aim." God, please rescue us from those things that are not real and eternal. No GPA, no scholastic accolade, no prestigious university, no desire to grow up to make a name for themselves, no athletic accomplishment, no promise of a high-paying career, no Broadway show standing ovation will grant peace, hope, or salvation. Daily pointing our children to eternity should be our great desire because Christ is their and our only hope.

## OUR APPARENT PRIVILEGE

As parents, we have an incredible privilege to point our children to Christ and model His grace before them daily. Don't give that privilege to a pastor or youth pastor. It is yours alone. My prayer for you now that you have read this book is that you have gained a glimpse of the eternal and the unparalleled privilege you have before your eyes every day.

I can't say it any better than the prayer in 2 Thessalonians 2:16–17: "Now may our Lord Jesus Christ himself, and God our Father, who loved us and gave us eternal comfort and good hope through grace, comfort your hearts and establish them in every good work and word." That is my prayer for you.

I pray the same grace that every prodigal and believer needs will bring hope and comfort to your heart. I pray you never lose sight of the grace you have to point your children toward the eternal and model the Gospel every day before our children.

This is our task.

This is our apparent privilege.

And I thank God for His grace to lead us through.

# NOTES

Chapter 1:
1. Wayne Rice and David Veerman, *Understanding Your Teenager* (Lakeside, CA: Understanding Your Teenager Books, 1999) p. 118.
2. Taken from www.MVParents.com, a Web site of the Coors Brewing Company.
3. Southern Baptist Convention survey, taken from www.sbcstudents. com/annualsurvey/2007ParentYouthRelationships.pdf.
4. Information taken from an article entitled "MTV and the Associated Press Release Landmark Study of Young People and Happiness" found at www.mtv.com/thinkmtv/research/.
5. Taken from www.familytalkonline.com/docs/AboutUs.htm.
6. Bob Altemeyer and Bruce Hunsberger, *Amazing Conversions* (Amherst, NY: Prometheus Books, 1997) p. 10.
7. Ibid, p. 226.
8. Merton Strommen and Richard Hardel. *Passing on the Faith: A Radical New Model for Youth and Family Ministry* (Winona, MN: Saint Mary's Press, 2000) p. 304.
9. Josh McDowell, *The Last Christian Generation* (Holiday, FL: Green Key Books, 2006) p. 60.
10. Steve Farrar. *King Me: What Every Son Wants and Needs from His Father* (Chicago: Moody Publishers, 2005) pp. 20–21.
11. This survey was conducted during summer of 2008. The informal survey was conducted of middle and high school students in a camp setting as they self-reported anonymously on survey forms. You can find more results from the survey on www.lastingdivergence.com.
12. John Angell James, "Religious Education of Children, a New Year's Address to Parents and Ministers," inserted in the *Evangelical Magazine*, January 1846.

Chapter 2:
13. Paul David Tripp, *War of Words* (New Jersey: P&R Publishing, 2000) p. 7.

14. National Coalition for the Protection of Families and Children, study of teens in New York and New Jersey (1999).

15. Internet search on Google, conducted March 3, 2008.

16. Taken from www.kff.org/entmedia/entmedia110905pkg.cfm.

17. Center for Communication and Social Policy, University of California, Santa Barbara (UCSB), National Television Violence Study, Executive Summary, vol. 3 (1998). Downloaded as "Key Facts: TV Violence" (Document #3335) from www.kff.org.

18. Mark Regnerus, *Forbidden Fruit: Sex and Religion in the Lives of American Teenagers* (New York: Oxford Press, 2007) p. 4.

19. Steve Farrar, *King Me: What Every Son Wants and Needs from His Father* (Chicago: Moody Publishers, 2006) p. 167.

20. David Kinnaman, *UnChristian: What a New Generation Really Thinks about Christianity* (Grand Rapids: Baker Books, 2007) p. 44.

21. Ibid, p. 47.

22. Taken from: www.asne.org/kiosk/reports/97reports/journalists90s/profiles5.html.

23. Kinnaman, p. 44.

24. Taken from www.foxnews.com/story/0,2933,311318,00.html.

25. Gallup Poll, "What's Morally Acceptable?" June 22, 2004.

26. Marilyn Elias, "Study Pinpoints Factors for Early Sex" *USA Today*, November 12, 2007.

27. From the article "Pew Forum on Religion & Public Life Releases Results from a Landmark Survey on Religion in the U.S." taken from: www.foxbusiness.com/article/pew-forum-religion-public-life-releases-results-landmark-survey-religion_493124_1.html.

28. Ibid.

29. Thom Rainer, *The Bridger Generation* (Nashville: Broadman & Holman, 1997) p. 163.

30. http://www.family.org/faith/A000000404.cfm.

31. Taken from: www.smh.com.au/news/world/the-most-popular-name-mohammed/2007/12/20/1197740468204.html.

32. Kinnaman, p. 25.

33. Mark Senter, *The Coming Revolution in Youth Ministry* (Wheaton, IL: Victor Books, 1992) p. 142.

34. David Bakan, "Adolescence in America: From Idea to Social Fact" as published in *Adolescent Behavior: Readings and Interpretations* (New York: McGraw-Hill Books, 2001) pp. 4–16.

35. Christian Smith, taken from www.christianitytoday.com/ bc/2007/006/2.10.html.

36. Ibid.

37. Taken from www.money.cnn.com/2006/12/29/magazines/moneymag/ boomerangkids.moneymag/index.htm.

38. Kinnaman, p. 22.

39. George Barna, *Revolutionary Parenting* (Wheaton, IL: BarnaBooks/ Tyndale House, 2007) pp. 11–12.

40. Search Institute. Taken from www.search-institute.org/families/In-fluenceofParents.pdf.

41. Ed Gamble interview with the *Texan*, taken from: www.exodusman-date.org/art_priority_of_kingdom_education_begins_by_starting.htm.


Chapter 3:

42. Taken from www.absconsulting.com/resources/Catastrophe_Reports/ Izmit-Turkey-1999.pdf.

43. Ibid.

44. CNN Headline News, June 8, 2008.

45. Micah Gamino, "More couples deciding not to tie the knot," *The Okla-homan*, Feb. 11, 2008, taken from www.newsok.com/article/3203121/.

46. Taken from www.findarticles.com/p/articles/mi_m4021/is_2001_ Nov_1/ai_79501204.

47.Taken from www.dailymail.co.uk/femail/article-495495/Meet-women-wont-babies--theyre-eco-friendly.html.

48. Taken from www.washingtonpost.com/wp-dyn/content/arti-cle/2008/06/07/AR2008060701531.html?hpid=moreheadlines.

49. Taken from www.foxnews.com/story/0,2933,141198,00.html.

50. Jennifer Baker of the Forest Institute of Professional Psychology in Springfield, Missouri. Taken from www.divorcerate.org.

51. George Barna statistic taken from www.christianpost.com/arti-cle/20080404/31815_Study:_Christian_Divorce_Rate_Identical_to_Na-tional_Average.htm.

52. As reported by Al Mohler. Taken from www.albertmohler.com/blog_read.php?id=794.

53. Taken from www.nytimes.com/2007/01/27/business/27instincts.html.

54. I am indebted to Dr. Jimmy Scroggins, senior pastor of First Baptist West Palm Beach, for my understanding of these concepts. The material in these pages is in large part from my conversations with him.

55. Randy Stinson, from the CBMW Journal, taken from www.cbmw.org/Journal/Vol-6-No-1/Executive-Director-s-Column.

56. Taken from www.foxnews.com/story/0,2933,355836,00.html.

57. John Angell James, "Religious Education of Children, a New Year's Address to Parents and Ministers," inserted in the *Evangelical Magazine*, January 1846.

Chapter 4:

58. Taken from www.religioustolerance.org/chr_dira.htm.

59. Taken from www.prb.org/Articles/2001/WhatChildrenLearnFromDivorce.aspx.

60. From the article "Cost of children? The numbers ain't kidding" Found at www.msnbc.msn.com/id/20203458/.

61. Taken from: www.thechristianmomsoutlet.wordpress.com/2008/01/13/children-are-a-blessing-from-the-lord/.

62. John Angell James, "Religious Education of Children, a New Year's Address to Parents and Ministers," inserted in the *Evangelical Magazine*, January 1846.

Chapter 5:

63. J. C. Ryle, "The Duties of Parents," taken from www.anglicanlibrary.org/ryle/parents.

64. Dr. Wes Black, as quoted in "Stopping the Dropouts" InQuest Insight article, March 2008.

65. The National Center on Addiction and Substance Abuse at Columbia University, "Malignant Neglect: Substance Abuse and America's Schools" (2001). Notes 3–6 were found at www.pmusa.com/en/prc/facts/research.asp.

66. Simantov et al., "Health-Compromising Behaviors: Why do adolescents smoke or drink?" Archives of *Pediatric and Adolescent Medicine* (2000).

67. The National Center on Addiction and Substance Abuse at Columbia University, "The Importance of Family Dinners" (2003).

68. The National Center on Addiction and Substance Abuse at Columbia University, "National Survey of American Attitudes on Substance Abuse VI: Teens" (2001).

69. Taken from www.search-institute.org/families/InfluenceofParents.pdf.

70. Von Salisch, M. "Children's emotional development: Challenges in their relationships to parents, peers, and friends," *International Journal of Behavioral Development* (2001) pp. 25, 310–319.

71.Gary Thomas, *Sacred Parenting* (Grand Rapids: Zondervan, 2004) p. 15.

Chapter 6:

72. Robert Clark, Joanne Brubaker, and Roy Zuck, *Childhood Education in the Church* (Chicago: Moody Press, 1986) p. 33.

73. George Barna, *Revolutionary Parenting* (Carol Stream, IL: Tyndale House Publishers, 2007) pp. 11–12.

74. Dr. Tom Ascol, taken from www.cbmw.org/Resources/Articles/Family-Worship.

75. Christian Smith, *Soul Searching* (Oxford University Press, 2005) p. 267.

76. Mark DeVries, "The Role of Parents in Kids' Spiritual Formation," *Youth Worker*, March/April 2003, p. 22.

77. Taken from abcnews.go.com/GMA/story?id=1375842&page=1.

78. Josh McDowell, *The Last Christian Generation* (Holiday, FL: Green Key Books, 2006) p. 13.

79. Mark Matlock, "From Wacky to Wise" *Youth Workers Journal*, May/June 2006.

80. George Barna, *Real Teens* (Ventura, CA: Regal Books, 2001) p. 136.

81. Glen Schultz, taken from www.KingdomEducation.com.

82. Jeremy and Jerusha Clark, *After You Drop Them Off: A Parent's Guide to Student Ministry* (Colorado Springs: Waterbrook Press, 2005) p. 192.

83. Josh Harris, *Stop Dating the Church!* (Sisters, OR: Multnomah Publishers, 2004) p. 31.

84. George Barna, *Revolutionary Parenting*, p. xvii.

85. Ibid., p. 106.

86. Clark, Brubaker, and Zuck, p. 33.

Chapter 7:

87. James C. Rodríguez, "Do Fathers Make a Difference: Social and Public Policy as a Catalyst for Responsible Fatherhood," Fathers & Families Coalition of America, Inc. (2007) p. 2, found at www.azffc.org/files/Whitepaper%20on%20Fatherhood%20Policies.doc.

88. Jareb Collins, "Latchkey Kids: An American Epidemic," found at: www.associatedcontent.com/article/73413/latchkey_kids_an_american_epidemic.html.

89. Susan Logue, "Millions of Children Raised by Grandparents" found at: www.voanews.com/english/archive/2006-09/2006-09-20-voa58.cfm?C-FID=30641002&CFTOKEN=84922281.

90. Richard Ross, taken from a promotional mailing, posted at www.lastingdivergence.com/?p=249.

91. Statistics referenced in Chapter 6, notes 6–11.

92. Ligon Duncan, taken from: www.spurgeon.wordpress.com/2007/08/10/family-worship-with-little-children/

93. John Piper, taken from www.desiringgod.org/ResourceLibrary/Articles/ByDate/1995/1560_The_Family_Together_in_Gods_Presence.

94. David Horner, *Firmly Rooted, Faithfully Growing Principle-Based Ministry in the Church* (2001) p. 58.

95. Nancy Leigh DeMoss, taken from www.reviveourhearts.com/topics/article.php?lid=20929.

96. Between 63 and 66 percent of children reported this was true. Search Institute, "Effective Christian Education: A National Study of Protestant Congregations: Summary Report" (Minneapolis, 1990) p. 46.

97. Search Institute, "Congregation at Crossroads: A National Study of Adults and Youth in the Lutheran Church Missouri Synod" (Minneapolis, 1996) p. 21.

98. David Cohen, all the information from this paragraph was taken from www.hrsbstaff.ednet.ns.ca/waymac/Sociology/A%20Term%201/2.%20Culture/Rituals.htm.

99. Suggested resources for Passage Trips and Journey Days are: Randy Stinson at www.CBMW.org, Robert Lewis's *Raising A Modern-Day Knight*, Brian D. Molitor's *Boy's Passage, Man's Journey*, Steve Farrar's

*King Me*, John Eldredge's *The Way of the Wild Heart,* John and Staci Eldredge's *Captivating,* Annie Chapman's *10 Things I Want My Daughter to Know,* Steve Chapman's *10 Things I Want My Son to Know,* Rick Johnson's *Better Dads, Stronger Sons,* Meg Meeker's *Strong Fathers, Strong Daughters,* Carolyn and Nicole Mahaney's *Girl Talk: Mother-Daughter Conversations on Biblical Womanhood* and blog at www.girltalk.blogs.com.

100. Nancy Gibbs, "The Magic of the Family Meal," *TIME* magazine, June 4, 2006. Taken from: www.time.com/time/magazine/article/0,9171,1200760,00.html.

101. Ibid.

102. David and Kathy Lynn, *Home Grown Faith* (Nashville: World Publishing, 2006) p. 26.

103. An example of research from the National Center on Addiction and Substance Abuse at Columbia University can be found at www.casafamilyday.org/PDFs/2005/10Benefits.pdf.

104. Found in the *Atlanta Journal-Constitution*, December 21, 1994, and *Fort Worth Star-Telegram*, December 21, 1994, p. 6.

Chapter 8:

105. Rick Johnson, *Better Dads, Stronger Sons* (Grand Rapids: Fleming H Revell Books, 2006) p. 38.

106. U.S. Department of Health and Human Services, Bureau of the Census. Notes 2–9 are from "Getting Men Involved" (Spring 1997) found at www.FatherMag.com/news/1780-stats.shtml.

107. FatherMag and Centers for Disease Control.

108. FatherMag and Centers for Disease Control.

109. FatherMag and Criminal Justice & Behaviour (1978) vol.14, pp. 403–26.

110. FatherMag and National Principals Association Report on the State of High Schools.

111. FatherMag and Rainbows for All God's Children.

112. FatherMag and U.S. Dept. of Justice, Special Report (Sept. 1988).

113. FatherMag and Fulton Co. Georgia Jail Populations and Texas Dept. of Corrections (1992).

114. Taken from www.childwatch.bm/documents/Father%20Mother%20 Child%20Facts.pdf.
115. John Stonestreet, Summit Ministries, "Five Reasons Why Students Walk Away from Their Faith," 2006 IAHE Conference, Indianapolis, IN, March 24, 2006.
116. Rick Johnson, p. 30.
117. Michael Harris, *What a Daughter Needs from Her Dad* (Minneapolis: Bethany House, 2004) p. 18.
118. Steve Farrar, *King Me* (Chicago: Moody Publishers, 2005) p. 15.
119. James Dobson, *Solid Answers* (Wheaton: Tyndale House Publishers, 1997) p. 92.
120. John Angell James, "The Christian Father's Present to His Children" (1825) taken from www.gracegems.org/21/christian_father2.htm.
121. Study by Work Foundation, British Telecommunications and Management Today, found at: www.findarticles.com/p/articles/mi_qn4158/ is_20031222/ai_n12718002.
122. John Piper, *Don't Waste Your Life* (Wheaton: Crossway Books, 2003) p. 32.
123. John Owen, referenced at blogs.sovgracefairfax.org/cross-roads/2006/09/22/are-you-killing-sin/.
124. Information taken from Jeff Myers, *Handoff: The Only Way to Win the Race of Life* (Dayton, TN: Legacy Worldwide Books, 2008) pp. 45–47.

Closing:
125. John Angell James, "Young Man Leaving Home" (1844) found at www.gracegems.org/21/young_man_leaving_home13.htm.
126. Edward Markquart. Taken from a sermon on Luke 15 which can be found at: www.sermonsfromseattle.com/series_c_lost_sheep_coin_son_ GA.htm.
127. "Come Thou Fount of Every Blessing" by Robert Robinson (1757), public domain.
128. Abraham Piper, "12 Ways to Love Your Wayward Child," copyright Desiring God (2007), found at: www.desiringgod.org/ResourceLibrary/ TasteAndSee/ByDate/2007/2168_12_Ways_to_Love_Your_Wayward_ Child, pp. 4–5.

# OTHER RESOURCES AVAILABLE

## ApParent Privilege
## Parent Curriculum

Based on Steve Wright's book of the same title, *ApParent Privilege Parent Curriculum* is a 4-week study created to exhort and encourage parents in their role as primary disciplers of their children. It will equip you with everything you need to present the concepts in *ApParent Privilege* to a small group, Sunday School class or in a parent meeting." (PDF Format)

Session 1: Our God-Given Privilege
Session 2: Our Guiding Principles
Session 3: Our Gospel-Centered Priorities
Session 4: Our Daily Practices

## reThink:
## Decide for Yourself – Is Student Ministry Working?

Is student ministry accomplishing what we think it is? Roughly two-thirds of students leave the church after graduation. Baptisms are down. Student pastors are walking away from ministry at startling rates. It's time to rethink student ministry. This book pairs the most up-to-date research available with an overview of a biblical framework for ministry. It will arm pastors and leaders with facts, Scripture, and real-life ideas that will help you find new ways to involve parents back into the equation and help you escape the busy, bigger-and-better, number-driven model of student ministry. This book is written for church pastors, teachers, and volunteers and is the companion to *ApParent Privilege*.

## HELP! I'm a Minister's Wife!

Author Tina Wright combines 134 survey responses and her fourteen years of experience as a minister's wife to present an honest, probing look into the lives of women serving alongside their husbands in ministry. Issues addressed include criticism, loneliness, expectations, genuine friendships, and meeting husbands' needs. *Help! I'm a Minister's Wife!* is a book designed to encourage every pastor's wife in her role as well as strengthen her marriage and ministry.

To order these resources and more visit
**www.inquest.org**

# ABOUT THE AUTHORS

Steve Wright and his wife, Tina, were married in 1989. They are blessed with three children: Sara, William, and Tyler. Steve graduated from Carson-Newman College, and he received a Master of Arts in Christian Education from New Orleans Baptist Theological Seminary. He completed his Ph.D. in Family Ministries at the Southern Baptist Theological Seminary in Louisville, Kentucky in 2013. Steve served in student and family ministry for over twenty-five years including 13 years at Providence Baptist Church in Raleigh, North Carolina (during which he wrote this book). He is currently serving at First Baptist Church of West Palm Beach, FL as Pastor of Discipleship and Church Planting. Steve founded InQuest Ministries out of his desire to equip and serve student pastors. He is also the author of *reThink: Decide for Yourself – Is Student Ministry Working?*.

Chris Graves and his wife, Anne, live in Knoxville, Tennessee, with their three boys: Wyatt, Rex and Judd. Chris has served in student ministries since 1997. Chris has also written youth ministry curriculum for InQuest Ministries, where he co-authored *reThink* with Steve Wright, and Emerald Youth Foundation, an urban ministry in Knoxville. He is a graduate of Carson-Newman College and Southeastern Baptist Theological Seminary.

30420153R00098

Made in the USA
Lexington, KY
09 February 2019